RAISING
YOUR
CHILD TO
LOVE GOD

BOOKS BY ANDREW MURRAY

The Blood of Christ
Mighty Is Your Hand (edited by Hazard)
Raising Your Child to Love God
Revival
Waiting on God

ANDREW MURRAY CHRISTIAN MATURITY LIBRARY

The Believer's Absolute Surrender
The Believer's Secret of Holiness
The Believer's Secret of Spiritual Power (with Finney)
The Spirit of Christ

ANDREW MURRAY PRAYER LIBRARY

The Believer's Prayer Life
The Believer's School of Prayer
The Ministry of Intercessory Prayer

WHAT the BIBLE TEACHES
ABOUT PARENTING

RAISING
YOUR
CHILD TO
LOVE GOD

A SPIRITUAL CLASSIC FROM
ANDREW MURRAY

BETHANYHOUSE
Minneapolis, Minnesota

Published by Bethany House Publishers
A Ministry of Bethany Fellowship International
11400 Hampshire Avenue South
Bloomington, Minnesota 55438
www.bethanyhouse.com

Printed in the United States of America by
Bethany Press International, Bloomington, Minnesota 55438

Library of Congress Cataloging-in-Publication Data

Murray, Andrew, 1828-1917.
    Raising your child to love God : what the Bible teaches about parenting / by Andrew Murray.
       p. cm.
    Rev. ed. of: How to raise your children for Christ. 1975.
    ISBN 0-7642-2462-X (pbk.)
    1. Christian education—Sermons. 2. Christian education—Home training.
I. Murray, Andrew, 1828–1917. How to raise your children for Christ. II. Title.
BV1477 .M8   2001
248.8'45—dc21   00-012101

ANDREW MURRAY was born in South Africa in 1828. After receiving his education in Scotland and Holland, he returned to South Africa and spent many years there as both pastor and missionary. He wrote over two hundred books, including some of the most enduring classics of Christian literature. He and his wife, Emma, raised eight children, and it is said that their home was an endless stream of activity.

PREFACE

God is awakening in many hearts the longing to live a truly consecrated life, to be and do all that He would have us do. No sooner has the surrender to such a life taken place but the desire comes to have all who belong to us partake of the blessing too—especially to have our homes and our families reflect our consecration to God. Many parents may find this a difficult task, even impossible in this day and age.

At the time when their own Christian life was halfhearted and wanting, the spirit of the world may have come in and caused them to pursue a life far from God's best for them. If there is a spouse or children who do not entirely sympathize with a renewed spiritual life, the one making the consecration will find it even more difficult to maintain, and will have the added challenge of seeking to emulate Christ to indifferent family members.

To parents who find themselves in this position, and to all parents who long to have their homes truly consecrated by God's presence and yielded to His service, God's Word has a message of comfort and strength: "Now to him who is able to do immeasurably more than all we ask or imagine, according to his power that is at work within us, to him be glory in the church and in Christ Jesus throughout *all generations*, for ever and ever!" (Ephesians 3:20). God is willing to be Lord of our families, and by His power He will do more than we can imagine. If we open our hearts in faith and rest on the promises and power of

God, He will prove himself to be for our loved ones what He has been for us.

Parents must know and believe what God longs to be and to do for their offspring. They will find that the lessons they learned embarking on a life of entire consecration are what are needed as they seek to bring their children to a commitment to Christ. All is realized in the word *surrender*.

This surrender of faith must also take place with regard to the family. As a parent, I put myself *and* my children into God's hands, believing that He will fulfill His promises—that He will accept my commitment and take control. I repent of the sins that have prevented God from working through me as He would like to in my home. I yield myself to be His humble witness, His obedient servant, and a faithful example to my children.

A parent's faith for his or her children is the same kind of faith exercised for personal trust in Christ. When we know and have experienced His working in our life, it is that much easier to trust Him for our children.

It is my hope that this book will help believing parents to meditate on God's purposes for the family and to see what abundant ground there is for expecting Him to fulfill their desire to have a home that glorifies the Lord. It is as we get into the mind and plan of God that faith will grow and its power will be manifested both in our lives and in the lives of those we love.

Andrew Murray
(1828–1917)

CONTENTS

Principles of Training

There are principles upon which all training rests.

First, meditate carefully and prayerfully on what training implies: it is a work that cannot be performed without careful thought and earnest purpose. And upon deep reflection, the infinite significance of the holy work of molding, forming, and giving shape to an immortal spirit causes us to plead the promise: "If any of you lacks wisdom, he should ask God, who gives generously to all without finding fault, and it will be given to him" (James 1:5).

1. *Training is more than teaching.* Teaching makes a child know and understand what is expected of him; training influences him and follows through to see that he does what he is asked. Teaching deals with his mind; training, with his will.

2. *Prevention is better than cure.* True training is not to watch and correct mistakes but to watch and *prevent* mistakes. To lead the child to know that she *can* obey and do right, that she can do it easily and successfully, and to delight in doing it, is the highest aim of true training.

3. *Habits must precede principles.* Habits influence the person by giving a certain bent and direction, by making the performance of certain actions easy and natural, and thus preparing the way for obedience by principle.

4. *The cultivation of the feelings precedes that of the judgment.* The early years of childhood are marked by the effervescence of feelings and the susceptibility of impressions. Parents seek to cre-

ate favorable feelings toward the good, to make goodness attractive and desirable. Without this, encouraging good habits will have little value.

5. *Example is better than precept.* The power of training lies not in what we say and teach but in what we *are* and *do*. We train our children not by *talking about* ideals and lofty goals but by *living* these out before them. It is not merely our strong desires or theories but our will and our practice that actually do the training. It is by living the Christ-life that we prove that we love Christ and that we are His true followers, and in this way we will influence young minds to love Christ and to live for Him too.

6. *Love that draws is more important than law that demands.* Training children calls for a life of self-sacrifice, of love that seeks not its own but lives and gives itself for its object. For this God has given incomparable mother-love: it only needs to be directed into the right channels. Law alone always works sin and wrath. Love gives itself by thought and strength to live for and in the other and breathes its own stronger and better life into the weaker one. Love inspires, and it is inspiration that is the secret of training.

Among the first traits of a heavenly spirit in the child is restfulness. The following remarks[1] on cultivating this, even during the first two years of a child's life, are well worth thoughtful perusal:

> We may even from the earliest infancy cultivate those dispositions which are unfavorable to the growth of dangerous inclinations. Certain habits, which exercise a salutary influence on the moral feelings, may be given to the infant even before his character distinctly shows itself. Inward tranquility will calm the restlessness of his wishes, and the kindness bestowed upon him will direct his attention out of him-

[1]Taken from Madame Necker de Saussure, *Progressive Education*, publisher and date unknown.

self and make him feel kindly toward others.

Inward tranquility is produced by outward tranquility; and for this, among other reasons, infants should, as much as possible, be prevented from crying excessively. By a careful attention in this and other things we may keep the minds of children in a state of habitual tranquility, an inestimable advantage—easily lost, indeed, but perhaps the quality of all others most necessary to their moral constitution, as yet so weak and vacillating. Their nerves, once agitated, are long in recovering their tone, and both the health and character suffer in consequence. I do not dwell on this merely as a means of preventing evil. There is one entire class of qualities, the noblest of any, which will grow and ripen only in the shade of repose; in this class are not only included our virtues but also our most valuable acquirements. There is nothing worthy of admiration, nothing great in our moral nature, which is not cherished by serenity of mind. Why is it that this disposition, which seems to establish a connection between the soul and heaven, which can exist only when the heart is at peace with itself and all around it, is now so rarely to be found among us? Whatever the reason may be, we shall always find this happy disposition of mind in young children unless we ourselves are so unfortunate as to disturb it.

I have often thought that we are too accustomed to keeping infants constantly in motion. We certainly ought not to allow them to grow weary—[boredom] is the lethargy of the soul; but nothing is more likely to produce this evil than an excess of variety in our methods of amusing them. The more tranquility a child has enjoyed in infancy, the more he will possess hereafter; and a calm cheerfulness of disposition may be permanent, while merriment and glee seldom are. It is for this reason that it is so much more desirable for children to be occupied with things than with people; things are tranquil objects that do not interest them too eagerly. With people their feelings of sympathy or dislike are continually excited.

Chapter 1

The Family As God Created It

"So God created man in his own image, in the image of God he created him; male and female he created them. God blessed them and said to them, 'Be fruitful and increase in number; fill the earth and subdue it.' "

—Genesis 1:27–28

God's purpose in the creation of man was to reveal to the universe His own unseen glory and perfection. He was to have not only single points of resemblance to God but was also to prove that he was indeed created in God's image and after His likeness.

The traits of that likeness are varied and most wonderful. In the dominion he was to have over the earth, man was to exhibit the power of God as king and ruler of the universe. In the wondrous mental powers with which he was endowed, fitting him for this work, there was to be seen the image of God as the all-wise. In his moral powers there was to be some reflection of the light that is inaccessible and full of glory; God's righteousness and holiness were to be revealed.

But then there still remained one trait of the divine perfection, the very highest to be set forth: love. As infinite love, God lives not for himself but finds all His joy in imparting His own life to His children. In His heart He carries the Son of His love, begotten of the Father from eternity. As the loving one, He is the fountain of life; as the living one, He is the fountain of love.

And of this fatherhood, the father of the earthly family is to be the image and the likeness. In the life he imparts to his child, in the image he sees reflected, in the unity of which he is conscious, in the loving care he exercises, in the obedience and the trust he sees given to himself, in the love in which family life finds its happiness, the home and the earthly father are the image of the heavenly.

What a solemn and blessed picture this truth gives us of the parental relationship. What a sanctifying influence the right comprehension of it would have upon its privileges and responsibilities. How much better, in the light of this divine origin and purpose of the family, can we understand and value our relationship to our children. And how, on the other hand, all our relationships with them would strengthen our obedience and our confidence toward the Father in heaven. We would see the reciprocal effect of the heavenly and the earthly homes on each other. Every deeper insight into the Father's love and the Father's home would elevate the home on earth and enlarge our expectations of the blessing God, who appointed it, will certainly bestow upon it. Every experience of the love and blessing of a home on earth can be as a ladder by which we rise up to meet the great Father-heart of God. "In the beginning God created the heavens and the earth." The two are in correspondence with each other—the home in heaven with the heavenly Father, which is the original of the home on earth with its earthly father.

Fatherhood in the likeness of God was to be the avenue of communication to another being of an immortal life, ever blessed, and the establishment of a home of love like the home in heaven. This was to have been the high privilege of man as God created him. But sin came in and ruined this perfect plan. How terrible is the curse and the power of sin! Through the father the child becomes a partaker of the sinful nature, and the father so often feels himself too sinful to be a blessing to his child; thus the home becomes a path to destruction rather than to eternal life.

But—blessed be God!—what sin destroyed, grace restores. And as in these meditations we follow God's revelation in regard to the family, we shall find that all the purpose and provision of God's grace point back to the restoration of what at creation was intended: two parents loving God and creating for their children a loving home and environment conducive to their proper care and training—a reflection of the home and the love of the Father in heaven.

Let every parent who feels conscious of his own shortcomings—and who longs for wisdom and grace to do the task entrusted to him—look back in faith and hope to the heavenly origin of family life. The God who created it has redeemed it, too, and creates it anew. He watches over it with tender interest—loving and blessing every parent who desires to be a minister of His holy purposes. If you desire this, begin by making God's thoughts your thoughts: the fatherhood and the family on earth is the image and the likeness of a heavenly original. Look to God as the author of your family life; count upon Him to give all that is needed to make it what it should be. Let His Father-heart and His Father-love be your confidence. As you know and trust Him, the assurance will grow that He is fitting you for making your home, in ever-increasing measure, the bright reflection of His own.

PRAYER OF CONSECRATION

O great and holy Creator of men, you have honored me with the wonderful relationship of parent and child—a precious life owing its sustenance to me. You have blessed me with the true happiness and divine joy of loving and being loved. You have placed me in an earthly home and family that is meant to be the image of our heavenly home, where the Father and the Son dwell in everlasting love.

O God, I humbly confess that I utter these words with shame. How little has the perfect love and joy, purity and brightness of heaven been reflected in the home you have given to my charge! How little have I understood my calling or truly aimed at the high ideal you have set before me! Father, forgive me.

Hear me, I pray, as I beseech you to guide my thoughts and to help me in the study of your Word that I may more fully realize what your purposes are for my parenting role on this earth, and to know with what interest and love you look on each home given over to your protection and guidance. Teach me to know you as my Father, that the study and the experience of that divine original after which the parent's heart was created may fit me to be a godly parent to my child. And let the Father's love and blessing rest on our home. Amen.

CHAPTER 2

THE FAMILY AS SIN MADE IT

"This is the written account of Adam's line. When God created man, he made him in the likeness of God. He created them male and female and blessed them. And when they were created, he called them 'man.' When Adam had lived 130 years, he had a son in his own likeness, in his own image; and he named him Seth."

—Genesis 5:1–3.

"Now Cain said to his brother Abel, 'Let's go out to the field.' And while they were in the field, Cain attacked his brother Abel and killed him" (Genesis 4:8).

God created man in His own likeness; Adam, after he had sinned, brought forth sons in his own likeness, after his image. In the former, we have the key to the mystery of the incarnation and redemption to eternal glory; in the latter, we have an example that shows why sin has such fearful and universal power.

Man's power to give life to others is one of the wonderful traits of God's likeness. When sin took over, that likeness was not extinguished but terribly defaced; man still had the power to bring forth sons, but in his own likeness. By one swift blow, sin, in conquering Adam, conquered the race. The parental relationship has become the strength of sin; when God restores it, it is the strength of grace.

If we want to realize the full significance of these words, "Adam . . . had a son in his own likeness, in his own image," we have only to study the story of his family. It will teach us lessons of deep importance with regard to the family affected by the Fall.

Let us note how the father's sin reappears and ripens in that of his child. The command "You shall love the Lord your God with all your heart . . . and your neighbor as yourself" sums up the will of God concerning us. Adam transgressed the first part of the commandment and in sinning cast off the love of God. His firstborn refused subjection to the second part and became the murderer of his own brother. Had Adam continued in the love of God, Cain no doubt would have loved his brother. With Adam's sin his nature became corrupted, and that nature was imparted to the son in his likeness. The child's sin was the fruit of the father's.

This is the first picture of family life that God gives us in His Word, and what a shadow it casts on the home. How often parents can trace in the sins and ill tempers of their children their own shortcomings and transgressions. The remembrance that their children have inherited their natures from them ought to humble them, make them very patient and gentle, as well as very earnest and wise in dealing with the little ones and leading them to seek what alone can cure and conquer this sinful strain—the grace and mercy of Jesus Christ.

Parents must realize that God visits the sins of the fathers on the children; it will urge and encourage them to believe that He will no less remember mercy to the fathers and make the children partakers of that too.

Let us note further how in that first child's sin we have the root and type of all sin. The first family had been destined of God to be the image of the bliss of heaven, the mirror of the life of love that reigns there. Sin entered, and instead of being the emblem and the gate of heaven, the family became the type and the portal of eternal separation from God. Instead of the love and help and happiness for which God had appointed our social relationships, envy and anger and hatred and murder render it a scene of terrible desolation.

The root of all sin is selfishness, separating us first from God and then from man. How early does it manifest itself in children. How continually does it come up in school and at play. How often it rises even against parents and refuses the love or obedience that is due.

Let believing parents study with care what the Word of God reveals of love as the new and great commandment, as the fulfilling of the whole law, as the way to our dwelling in God and God in us, and seek for nothing so earnestly as this: *the reign of love in the home.* Let them watch over every manifestation of a selfish or unloving spirit as a seed of the tree that bore such bitter fruit in Cain, and count no care or prayer too great to have it banished. Let them not be content—even if there are no visible outbreaks of evil in their young children—but let them be aware and root out the seeds that so often ripen later in life. Let them make it their aim that grace restores their family life to what God created it to be—a mirror and a foretaste of the grace and beauty of heaven.

"In his own image, after his likeness"—these words refer not only to the blessing lost in paradise and to the curse that came with sin but also to the grace that comes with redemption. It doesn't mean that by natural birth a believer can bear a child in his likeness, renewed again by the Spirit of God. But what nature cannot accomplish, prayer and a life of faith can obtain by virtue of the promise and the power of God.

As we seek to know the teaching of the Word of God concerning family life, we shall discover more clearly the blessed truth that to believing parents the promise is given that their child may be begotten again after their likeness, and that God will to this end use them as the instruments of His grace. To the prayer of faith, manifesting itself in the godly training of the child, the blessing has been secured in covenant: "I will be a God to you and to your seed." As faith and prayer claim the promise and the power of God, the influence of daily communion will make itself felt and there will go out from the consecrated lives of the parents a secret but mighty power to mold the lives of their children, either preparing them as vessels of grace or establishing and perfecting them in it.

And so we come to the blessed but solemn truth: Let parents be what they want their children to be. If they would keep them from the sin of Cain, who did not love his brother, let them take care to avoid the sin of Adam, who did not love his God enough to resist temptation. *Let parents lead a life marked by love to God and man*; this is the atmosphere in which loving children can be trained. Let all dealings with children be in love. Cross words, sharp reproof, impatient answers, all are infectious. Love demands and fears not self-sacrifice; time and thoughtful attention and patient perseverance are needed to train our children in the way of truth. When our children hear us speak of others, of friends or enemies, let the impression be the love of Christ. In all the communication of parents with each other, let mutual esteem and respect, tender consideration and willing self-forgetfulness prove to the children that love is possible among us.

Above all, let us remember that it is the love of God that is the secret of a loving home. It is where parents love the Lord their God with all their heart and strength that human love will be strengthened and sanctified. It is only the parents who are willing to live truly consecrated lives, entirely given up to God, to whom the promise and the blessing can come fully true. To make our home the nursery and the type and the foretaste of heaven, ordinary, halfhearted religion will not suffice. The love of God shed abroad in the heart and the home and the life by the Holy Spirit—this alone will transplant our home from the gates of paradise lost, where Adam dwelt with Cain, to within the paradise regained, where even amid the weakness of earth the image of the heavenly is seen and the home on earth is the likeness of the home above.

Prayer of Consecration

Blessed Lord God, we bow before you in deep humility. We desire to feel more deeply the terrible power of sin in ourselves and in our children, and the danger to which it exposes our beloved home. We come to confess how far we as parents have come short in that pure and holy love that you meant to be the beauty and the blessedness of family life. In our fellowship with you and with one another—our children and our fellowmen— O God, forgive us for our lack of love! And let not our children suffer through us as they grow up in our likeness! Deliver us, we pray, from the power of selfishness, and shed abroad your love in our hearts by the Holy Spirit.

Bless our children with the spirit of love. May we so walk before them in love that your Spirit may use our example and our life to conform them to your likeness. Give us a deep sense of our holy calling to train their immortal souls for you and for your glory. Inspire us with faith, with patience, with wisdom to train them aright—that our home on earth might be to them the pathway, the gateway to the Father's home in heaven!

Blessed Father, let us and our children be yours wholly and forever. Amen.

CHAPTER 3

THE FAMILY AS GRACE RESTORES IT

"The LORD then said to Noah, 'Go into the ark, you and your whole family, because I have found you righteous in this generation.'"

—Genesis 7:1

By faith Noah prepared an ark for the saving of his house, and he was made a witness to future ages that the faith of a believing, righteous parent obtains a blessing not only for himself but also for his children. The New Testament teaching that by faith Noah saved his house is in perfect accordance with what is recorded in Old Testament history: "Go into the ark, you and your whole family." Even Ham—who as far as personal character was concerned manifestly deserved to perish with the ungodly world—was saved from the flood for his father's sake and by his father's faith. This is proof that in God's sight the family is regarded as a unit with the father as head and representative; that parents and children are one, and that in the dispensation of grace, even as in the ministration of condemnation, it is on this principle that God will deal with the families of His people.

We know that it is on the basis of the fact that parents and children are one that sin has its awful power in the world. When Adam sinned, his whole posterity was made subject at once, as it were, to sin and death. And was not the Flood as well as the Fall a proof of it? We see the children of Seth immersed as deeply as the children of Cain, because Seth, too, was a son whom Adam had begotten in his likeness with a sinful nature to be handed down to his children. Is it not this nature that has given sin such universal power to a thousand generations? The family is sin's greatest stronghold; children inherit an evil bent from their parents. The unity of parents and children becomes the strength of sin.

Noah's deliverance from the Flood was to be the introduction to a new dispensation—the first great act of God's redeeming grace on behalf of a sinful world. In this act God manifested the great principles of the economy of grace: mercy in the midst of judgment; life through death; faith as the means of deliverance, the one channel through which the blessing comes. And further, it was at this time revealed that the family was to be a means of that grace.

The family had been sin's greatest ally, the chief instrument through which it acquired such universal dominion. This unit was now to be rescued from the domination of sin, to be adopted into the covenant of grace, to be consecrated and made subservient to the establishment of God's kingdom. How otherwise could the declaration "Where sin abounded, there did grace much more abound" be verified if sin *alone* had the power through the parents to secure dominion over the children? No, in this very thing we have one of the brightest displays of redeeming grace—that the relationship of parents and children, which had become the means for transmitting and establishing the power of sin, was in a much greater way to become the vehicle for extending the kingdom of God's grace. And though many ages would pass before the promised Seed of the woman would be born, yet in anticipation of that holy birth, the seed of God's people were to share in the blessing of their parents. It was on the strength of this hope that the children of righteous Noah were blessed along with their father.

Let believing parents understand and remember this: the father who is righteous in God's sight is dealt with not only as an individual but also in his relationship as a parent. When God blesses, He loves to bless abundantly; the blessing must overflow the house of His servant. For this temporal life and the supply of its many needs, the father must regard himself as the appointed channel through whom the blessings of nature and providence must reach the child. And he may count upon God's help. But the parental relationship has a nobler destiny: The believing father is to regard himself as the appointed channel for eternal life with its many blessings and steward of the grace of God to his children.

When once we understand this blessed truth and by faith accept God's word "You have I seen righteous before me in this generation," we shall be able to value the word that follows: "Go into the ark, you and your whole family." The seed of the righteous shall be blessed; the house of His servant God will bless. God gives the assurance that the ark in which the parent is to be saved is meant for his children too; it is for them as much as for him. The ark is to be the house of the family.

As the blessing is to come *for his sake*, so it is also *through his instrumentality*. It is not only a promise but also a command: "Go into the ark, you and your whole family." God will not deal with the house separate and apart from him; the parent has to bring the children into the ark.

And if the question comes up as to the power of a parent to lead his children into the ark as certainly as he goes in himself, the answer is simple and clear: "By faith Noah prepared an ark for the saving of his house." God always gives grace proportionate to the duty He requires. Let the believing parent live and act and pray with and for his children as one to whom "the ark" and its salvation is indeed the one aim and joy of life, and who is assured that his children are meant to be there with him. *Let him confidently trust God for the salvation of every child.* Let him in that spirit instruct and inspire his children. The children will grow up with the consciousness that to be with their father is to be with one who is in the ark—the blessing cannot be missed.

Dear parents, listen to the wonderful truth of which Noah is God's messenger to you: There is room for your child in the ark. The God who saves you expects you to bring your child with you. It is no longer enough to pray and *hope* that your child may be saved. Accept in faith the assurance that he *can* be, and act out in obedience the command that you are to bring him in with you.

To the question as to "how," let the answer be taken deeper to heart, "Go into the ark, you and all your whole family." Go in and *live* in the ark; bring up and train your children there, wholly separated from the world. God's blessing will use this training for their salvation. Abide in Christ, and let the child feel that to be near you is to be near Christ. Live in the power of the love and the redemption and the life of Christ; your home will be to the child the ark where Christ is known and found. If you have indeed heard the blessed word, "You have I seen righteous," let it teach you in the obedience of a joyous faith to fulfill the precept "Go into the ark, you and your whole family." May this word live in the heart of each believing parent.

PRAYER OF CONSECRATION

O Lord, my God, I have heard your message that since you have accepted me as righteous in your Son, you would have my children be found in this position too. I have heard your voice of grace, "Go into the ark, you and your whole family." Blessed be your name for the assurance this message offers a parent's heart: the salvation of his children.

Lord, open my eyes to see what your Word sets before me. Let me see in Noah the picture of a believing parent—walking with you, believing your Word, always obedient to your commands. Let me see in the ark the type of my blessed Lord Jesus, a sure and safe hiding place for me and for my child. Let me see in the saving of Noah's house the sure pledge of what will be given to every parent who trusts you for his children and obeys your voice to bring them in.

O God, give me grace, like your servant Noah, to so walk with you that you may see me righteous—to believe the promise of your grace, to obey your command and perform the work entrusted to me, that your blessing may abide on me and on my children. And may it all be to the glory of your holy name. Amen.

CHAPTER 4

THE CHILD OF THE COVENANT

"Then the word of the LORD came to him: 'This man will not be your heir, but a son coming from your own body will be your heir.' He took him outside and said, 'Look up at the heavens and count the stars—if indeed you can count them.' Then he said to him, 'So shall your offspring be.' Abram believed the LORD, and he credited it to him as righteousness."

—Genesis 15:4, 6

"And you are heirs . . . of the covenant" (Acts 3:25).

Three times God gave Abraham the promise that He would make of him a great nation, as the sand of the seashore in multitude. When God appeared to him the fourth time, Abraham poured out his complaint before God: "I remain childless. . . . You have given me no children; so a servant in my household will be my heir." In answer, the word of the Lord came to him, saying, "This man will not be your heir, but a son coming from your own body will be your heir." And then follow the memorable words, "[Abraham] believed the LORD, and he credited it to him as righteousness."

The great truth that this narrative sets before us is this: The promise and the gift on God's part and the reception and the birth of our children on our part is altogether a matter of faith, a matter in which God takes the deepest interest. It is especially *as a parent*, in reference to the promise of a child, that Abraham's faith is exercised and found well pleasing to God. In the power of faith, the natural longing for a child becomes the channel of wonderful fellowship with God, and the natural seed becomes the heir of God's promise and of spiritual blessing.

The *reason for* and the *meaning of* all this is easily found. In Noah, God had begun to acknowledge the validity of the oneness of parents and children in the dealings of grace, but it had been to little avail.

Immediately after the Flood Ham's wickedness was revealed, and it was not many years before the whole world had fallen into idolatry. The children of Noah had been born after the flesh. Before their birth God had not entered into covenant on their behalf. In character, they had become independent men before God made them partakers of Noah's blessing. With Abraham, He would deal otherwise; His way of dealing in covenant with His servants was to be advanced a distinct stage forward.

Everything leading up to Isaac's birth was to be a matter of God's revelation and man's faith. The covenant child was the object of God's care and the parents' faith. God took charge of the very forming of the child, watching over him in the womb and sanctifying him by His Word and by faith. Against nature and against hope, God by His promise awakened faith and expectation of a child in the hearts of his parents. For twenty-five years this faith had been tried and purified until Abraham's whole soul was at last filled with believing expectancy. The child was in truth an answer to prayer, a gift of God received by faith.

Abraham was sealed for God in the covenant of circumcision, opening the way for future blessing on his seed. By this God would teach us the importance of entering into covenant with God, even before the first hope of having children. We are all called to exercise Abraham's faith and to receive our children from God's hands. The children, then, are partakers of the covenant from birth. Even *before* birth, in the very first rising of hope, would God begin the great work of redeeming love by His Spirit. By this He would reveal to us how that wondrous power with which He has endowed man to give life and bring forth children after His image—the power that through sin was made the strength of Satan's kingdom—was again to be consecrated, and under God's own eye to be used for the extension of His kingdom and glory.

The Bible is full of what cannot otherwise be understood—of divine promise and interposition, of human activity and expectation—with regard to the birth of children. Everything concentrates on one great lesson: The fatherhood and childhood of this earth have divine promise, and everything connected with the relationship must be a matter of faith, a religious service holy to the Lord and well pleasing in His sight. If I would fully honor God, I must believe not only for myself but also for my children, grasping God's promises for them as well. If I would magnify the riches of God's grace, if I would with my whole nature and all my power be consecrated to God's service, and if I would accomplish the utmost possible within my reach for the advancement of His kingdom, it is especially in the role of a parent that I must believe and work.

God apparently thought a long time was necessary for the strengthening and ripening of his faith before Abraham received the promised child. This grace is a gift of supreme value, and cannot be attained but by a close walk with God and wholehearted surrender to His teaching and leading. The faith that was sufficient to justify Abraham was not sufficient to receive the blessing for his seed; his faith had to be further strengthened and purified for this. Faith must be in proportion to the promise.

Believing parents will discover that nothing so greatly quickens the growth of their faith as the reaching out after blessing for their children. They will feel a strong motivation for a life of entire devotion and uncompromising faith, enough for themselves and enough to impart to their children—in harmony with that law of the kingdom: "According to your faith be it unto you."

Abraham's story gives us the comforting assurance that God will give the grace to attain what we need. With great patience and long-suffering He led Abraham and Sarah until they were fit to accomplish His purposes. Then it could be said of them, "Abraham *believed*" and became the father of many nations, and "*through faith* Sarah received strength to conceive seed, and was delivered of a child. . . ." Even now, God—who has undertaken to sanctify His people, soul and body, and to fill them with His Spirit—will himself train them for the holy calling of believing parents. He will teach us how bringing children into the world and raising them to love God can become the highest exercise of our faith and the truest means of advancing our spiritual life and the interests of His kingdom.

As with Abraham, so with us, the promise of God and the power of faith are the wondrous links by which the natural seed becomes the heir of the spiritual blessing and the parental relationship one of the best schools for the life of faith. It is especially in a believing fatherhood that we can become conformed to the image not only of faithful Abraham but also of the Father in heaven.

PRAYER OF CONSECRATION

Blessed God and Father, what thanks shall we render to you for the wondrous revelation of your will in your servants Abraham and Sarah? You took the fatherhood and motherhood of earth into your covenant charge and keeping, did sanctify and bless them, that the seed of your people might indeed be holy to the Lord. Where sin abounded and manifested its awful power, you made grace to much more abound; and Abraham's child, the heir of sin and misery, you made the heir of the promise and its blessing. Blessed be your name forever!

Gracious God, open the eyes of your servants to see how

through the birth of your "Isaac," your dear Son, Jesus Christ, our own children have indeed been redeemed from the power of sin, and your promise comes to us larger and fuller than Abraham could ever have understood it. Teach us, and all Christian parents, to realize that if there is one thing in which you have a keen interest, in which you give abundant grace, in which you nurture and strengthen faith, it is in the great ministry of parenthood. O God, enlighten and sanctify our hearts to realize that the fruit of our body is the heir of your promise. And let our parentage, as it was for Abraham, be what binds us to you in worship and in faith. Amen.

CHAPTER 5

THE PROMISE OF THE COVENANT

"I will establish my covenant as an everlasting covenant between me and you and your descendants after you for the generations to come, to be your God and the God of your descendants after you."

—Genesis 17:7

"It is not the natural children who are God's children, but it is the children of the promise who are regarded as Abraham's offspring" (Romans 9:8).

We have here the first full revelation of the terms of God's covenant, of God's dealing in grace with Abraham, the father of all who believe. Here is the great foundation promise of what God calls "an everlasting covenant." God had already revealed himself to Abraham as his God and as the God who would give him a child. The thing that is new and remarkable here is the assurance that the covenant now to be established was to be with his seed as much as with himself: ". . . your God and the God of your descendants after you." It is this promise that has invested these words throughout all the generations of God's church with an imperishable interest. Let us see how entirely the same promise is for the child as for the parent.

The *matter* of the promise is the same in each case: *"I will establish my covenant . . . to be your God and the God of your de-*

scendants after you." It is God's purpose to stand in the same relationship to the child as the father stands; the believing parent and the innocent child are to have the same place before Him. God longs to take possession of children before sin gets its mastery; from birth—yes, even from before birth—He would secure them as His own and have the parents' heart and the parents' love sanctified and guided and strengthened by the thought that the child is His—". . . your God and the God of your descendants."

The *certainty* of the promise is the same. It rests on God's free mercy, on His almighty power, His covenant faithfulness. God's faithfulness to His purpose is the ground on which the promise rests and its fulfillment may be expected.

The *condition* of the promise is in each case the same. In its twofold blessing it is offered to *the faith* of the parent, and has to be accepted by faith alone. If the promise "I will be your God" is not believed, that unbelief makes the promise of none effect. God is true, His promise faithful, His offer of mercy real. But if it finds no entrance through unbelief, the blessing is lost. And so with the other half—"and the God of your descendants"—if the parent's faith accepts this for his child, God will see to it that his faith is not disappointed.

The *recipient* of the promise is the same. It is not as if the first half of the promise is given to the father and the second half to the child. Rather, the two parts are given to the parent, the first to accept for himself and the other part to accept on behalf of his child. The promise is not held in abeyance to wait for the child's faith, but is given to the father in the assurance that the child's faith will follow. With Abraham, as with each believing parent, the same faith accepts the personal and the parental blessing. The blessing is in either case equally sure if faith holds it equally firm.

But here a difficulty arises with many. They see that God's promises of mercy to sinners are free and sure, and have found, in believing them, that they have come true; they know that they have been accepted. But it is as if the promise with regard to the children is not equally simple and certain. They cannot understand how one can so confidently believe for another. They know that the only sure ground for faith is God's Word, but they have not yet been able to realize that the Word of God really means that He is the God of their offspring as well. Their impressions are in accordance with this ordinarily held view: "God has established a general connection between seedtime and harvest, between faithful parental training and the salvation of children. In neither case—the seedtime nor the training—is absolute certainty of success secured or God's sovereignty excluded. It is enough that the promise expresses the tendency and ordinary result of proper training."

It is evident that such a general principle, with its possible exceptions, cannot give the rest of faith that the parent longs for. Faith needs the assurance that God's purpose and promise are clear and unmistakable; then alone can it venture everything upon His faithfulness.

Such was the promise given to Abraham; such is the promise to every believing parent. It is not in the general law of seedtime and harvest that I am to find the parallel for my basis of hope on behalf of my child, but in the other very distinct and definite promise, "[I will] be your God," is the divine pattern and pledge of the second, "and the God of your descendants after you."

When as a struggling sinner I first sought for mercy, it was not to some general principle—seeking is generally followed by finding—that I trusted, but to the very definite divine assurance, "Everyone that asks receives, and he that seeks finds." I believed the promise; I came and was accepted; I found the promise true: "I will your God." So the promise is now brought that He is willing to be the God of my descendants too. Wherever God comes with a promise, He expects faith to accept it at once. The promise was not *conditional* on Isaac's believing but rather intended to be faith's source and security. And so as I stand in covenant with God as my God and see how He offers to be the God of His people's seed, I have the right in faith to claim this promise and to be assured of my child's salvation as firmly as my own, through faith in the God of truth.

The analogy between the two halves of the promise is complete. In the first, it was the question: Could I trust the love and power and faithfulness of God to accept and renew and keep such a sinner as I am? Faith gave the answer and secured the blessing. And now the other question: Can I trust the love and power and faithfulness of God to accept and renew and keep my child? Faith can again give the answer, and this blessing, too, is secured.

And if the thought should still come up, as it has come up and troubled many, *What about election? How can I be sure that my child is one of the elect?* The first half of the promise again gives the solution. When I believed to the saving of my soul, I was sure the election and the promise of God never could be at odds with each other. Even so with my child. No believer in God's promise ever complained that God's sovereignty hindered its fulfillment. "They that are the children of the flesh, these are not the children of God but the children of the promise.

The promise is definite: "a God unto you and your seed." Let us, like Abraham, falter not at the promise through unbelief but be strong in faith, giving glory to God, and be confident that what He has spoken He is able and faithful to perform. Let us look upon our children, let us love them and train them as children of the covenant and children of the promise—these are the children of God.

PRAYER OF CONSECRATION

O God, how shall I sufficiently adore you for the grace you have revealed in the promise of the covenant? As if it were not enough to take such unworthy sinners and make them your children, you offer to provide for their children too, and make the house of your servants the home of your favor and blessing. You meet them with the sure promise once given to your servant Abraham: "I will be your God and the God of your descendants after you." Blessed be your holy name!

And now, Lord, I beseech you, give me grace to take this promise and trust it with my whole heart. As sure as my confidence that you are my God and have accepted me, so confident may I be that you are the God of my children. As I yielded my sinful self to you, and you took me as your own, I give my children, sinful too, to you, and believe that you take them as your own. As I accepted your promise for myself, I accept it for them. Give me grace now to look upon them as you do, as children of the promise. May this be what gives me courage and hope for their training on earth and their portion in heaven. They are the children of the covenant, children of the promise. Faithful is He who promised, who also will do it. Amen.

CHAPTER 6

THE SEAL OF THE COVENANT

"You are to undergo circumcision, and it will be the sign of the covenant between me and you. For the generations to come every male among you who is eight days old must be circumcised, including those born in your household or bought with money from a foreigner—those who are not your offspring."
—Genesis 17:11–12

Abraham received the sign of circumcision as a seal of the righteousness of faith. Such was the meaning, according to the teaching of the Holy Spirit, of the ordinance of circumcision given to Abraham. And yet there are many who speak of it as if it were only the initiatory rite into the temporal privileges of the Jewish people—as if it meant one thing to him, something deeply spiritual and sacred, and something else to his descendants! The whole argument of the epistle to the Romans reproved the Jews for looking at it in so carnal a light and degrading it from what it originally was: the holy sacrament of friendship and fellowship with God, the seal of the righteousness of faith, the emblem of the covenant of the spirit in which God would circumcise the heart, the sure sign of God's faithfulness to Abraham and to his offspring. There was no need in the New Testament for repeating in express words the truth, deeply inwrought into the life of God's people, that their children were as truly in the covenant and had as sure a right to its sign as they did. May the Holy Spirit lead us to know the mind of God.

We are taught that circumcision was a seal of the righteousness of faith. A seal is the confirmation of something that has been settled and transacted, the securing of privileges that have already been secured. Abraham believed, and God counted his faith to him as righteousness and took him into a covenant of friendship. Circumcision was to him a divine seal and assurance of this. But it was also a sign, and not an arbitrary one, with a spiritual meaning. It was a sign of the purity and holiness that was to be the mark of God's people.

The most remarkable feature of the covenant was the passing on of the blessing from generation to generation, taking possession for the service of God's kingdom the very power of generation. Of this power sin had taken possession; the very first sign of sin with Adam and Eve was that they knew they were naked and were ashamed. The fountain of life was defiled and had to be cleansed. So when the male child of eight days suffered the removal of the foreskin of his flesh, it was in recognition of the defilement there is in all flesh at birth; a foreshadowing of the One to come, begotten of the Holy Spirit, and of that second birth to be experienced in Him, not of the will of the flesh, but of God, the blessing of the new covenant. It was a type of the circumcision that is not made with hands: the putting off of the body of the flesh in the circumcision of Christ, being buried with Him in baptism. The *seal* of the righteousness of faith under the Old Testament was the *sign* of the need of regeneration, a sign for the quickening and instruction of Abraham's faith and his being set apart as a father for the service of God.

Circumcision could not be to the infant Isaac essentially different from what it was to Abraham. It was to him also a seal of his participation in that spiritual covenant of which God's promise and man's faith were the two marks. All unknowing, he had been taken, with his father and for his father's faith, into the

40

favor and covenant of God. It was to him, as to Abraham, a seal of faith, faith already existing and accepted—not his own, but his father's. For Abraham's sake the blessing came on him. We find this distinctly stated later on in Genesis 26:3, 5: "Stay in this land for a while, and I will be with you and will bless you . . . because Abraham obeyed me and kept my requirements, my commands, my decrees and my laws." And again in verse 24: "I am the God of your father Abraham. Do not be afraid, for I am with you; I will bless you and will increase the number of your descendants for the sake of my servant Abraham."

Abraham had not believed for himself alone but for his child; as a father he had believed and received the child in faith from God; the sign of circumcision in the child was the seal to the child of the father's faith. God dealt with father and child as one; the father believed for himself and his child as one; the child had the same place in the covenant and the same claim on the seal of the covenant as the father did. And as he grew up it would be to him a seal not only of the faith his father had but also of God's promise awaiting his faith—the reminder of the one thing required by God, the one thing well pleasing to Him and by which Isaac in turn could pass the blessing on to his own offspring.

What circumcision was to Abraham and Isaac, baptism is now to believers and their children. It, too, is a sign, only far clearer and brighter. If circumcision spoke of the shedding of blood and the purifying of the fountain of life, the water in baptism witnesses to the blood that has been shed and the Spirit that has been given, cleansing and renewing. "There are three who bear witness: the Spirit, and the water, and the blood." Of all these blessings it is a sign and also a seal—a seal from God of the righteousness of faith—faith in His promise that is well pleasing to Him and is counted as righteousness.

The parent must meet God as Abraham did—as a believer. It is faith and faith alone that can enter into the covenant—this pleases God and obtains the reward. He must believe in Christ for himself. Christ alone is the surety of the covenant; He is the covenant. And he must believe for his child: "Your God and the God of your seed"—these are the unchangeable terms of an everlasting covenant. The faith that claims the first may claim the second too. It has the same warrant—God's Word. It has the same hope—God's faithfulness. It obtains the same blessing of free grace—the salvation of my child as surely as my own.

PRAYER OF CONSECRATION

O God, we do thank you for the condescension to our weakness that you have shown in giving us in visible sign a divine seal of spiritual and unseen blessings. You know our frame and remember that we are dust. You are the Creator of our body and no less the Father of our spirit. You have redeemed our body to be the temple of your Holy Spirit. In the body you set the seal of your acceptance of us as well as your right over us. Lord, teach us to understand this; and let holy baptism, the seal of the New Testament faith and life, be to your people the sign that they are baptized into the death of Christ.

And grant, most gracious God, that where your people cannot yet see eye to eye in the dispensation of this ordinance it may still be the bond of unity in the Spirit of love and not the symbol of division.

And teach us to recognize the deep spiritual meaning in the seal of the covenant and to live as those who are baptized into the death of Christ, circumcised with a circumcision not made with hands. Teach us in faith to claim the full spiritual blessing for our children too, and to train them for it. And so fulfill to us, our God, in full measure, the promise of the covenant: "A God for you—and for your seed." Amen.

CHAPTER 7

KEEPING THE COVENANT

"For I have chosen him, so that he will direct his children and his household after him to keep the way of the LORD by doing what is right and just, so that the LORD will bring about for Abraham what he has promised him."
—Genesis 18:19

Faith without works is dead. Saving faith is *energy,* the power of a new life manifesting itself in conduct and action. In true faith the soul becomes united to God and seeks to enter into the divine will—the surest way of becoming one with Him. As faith grows clearer and stronger, it always sympathizes more fully with God's plans; it understands Him better, and becomes more conformed to His likeness. This is true not only of individual but also of parental faith. The higher the faith of the parent rises, the more the family will come under its power and be permeated by the spirit of godliness. Parental faith in God's promise will always be marked by parental faithfulness to God's will.

Abraham is a remarkable illustration of this. As distinctly as God's Word speaks of his faith, it tells, too, of his faithfulness as a father. In giving the reason why God's purpose in regard to Sodom should not be kept secret from him, He bases it upon this part of his character. God confers on him the high distinction of having His secret counsel revealed to him—not as an eminent believer, not even as the father of the promised seed, but as one called to be the faithful leader of his children and household in the ways of the Lord. Faithfulness in his household gave him access to God's secrets and to God's presence as intercessor for Sodom. Let's try to understand what this means and why God puts such honor upon parental faithfulness—let's look to its necessity, its character, its blessing, and its power.

First, think what *necessity* there is for this faithfulness. Without it the blessing offered to parental faith is lost and the purpose of God made void. Were God by direct interposition or by special agents to seek the salvation of the little ones, there would be no reason for the part the parent is allowed to take in the covenant. God's object in thus honoring the parent is distinctly that he, to whose influence the helpless child is committed, should train it for God. God seeks a people on earth to do His will. The *family* is the great institution for this object; a believing and God-devoted father is one of the mightiest means of grace. God's covenant and the parents' faith are but preliminary steps; it is through godly upbringing by the parents that children are led to enter upon and truly possess the blessings secured in the covenant. They must learn to know, to choose, and to love the God who gave himself for them. The most precious promises on God's part will not avail unless the child is brought up, in the course of patient and loving training, to desire and accept the proffered friendship of the Holy One, to obey Him and to keep His commandments. God establishes His covenant with parents not only for their comfort, to assure them of what He will do, but also to strengthen them for what they must do. They are His fellow workers in securing the children for Him.

What God says of Abraham gives us further insight into the true *character* of this grace: "For I have chosen him, so that he will direct his children and his household after him to keep the way of the LORD." The spirit of modern so-called liberty has penetrated even into our family life; and there are parents who, some from a mistaken view of responsibility, some from lack of thought as to their sacred calling, some from love of ease, have no place for such a word as "command." They have not seen the heavenly harmony between authority and love, between obedience and liberty. Parents are more than friends and advisers; God has clothed them with a holy authority to be exercised in leading their children in the way of the Lord. There is an age when the will of the child is to a great extent in their hands, and when the quiet, loving exercise of that authority will have mighty influence. We speak here not so much of commanding in the sense of specific injunctions, but rather of what we see in the heavenly Father—the tenderness of affection combined with an authority not to be despised. The silent influence of example and life also exercises its commanding power, making the child often unconsciously bow to the stronger will and even be happy in doing so.

The *blessing* of such parental faithfulness is sure and broad. In Abraham's case, the effectiveness of the covenant was brought about through a godly education for his son. So we see that God's faithfulness and man's faithfulness to the covenant obligation are linked by indissoluble ties, each performing his part. If Abraham was to be blessed, and his seed with him, and all nations in turn through his seed, it could only be by his being a faithful parent, passing on to his son what he had learned and knew of God. And it is only as children become partakers of the parents' spirit that they can share the blessing.

The solemn responsibility may well make us tremble. But God's Word meets us with divine comfort. The *power* is provided in the purpose of God. The words of the text are most remarkable: "For I have chosen [Abraham], so that he will direct his children and his household." It was with this very purpose that God had called him and revealed himself; God was the security that His own purposes should be carried out. And so every believing parent has, in the very fact of his being taken into this relation with God, the guarantee that God will give the grace of faithfulness to prepare for the blessing as well as the reward.

It is part of God's covenant that He will first teach man to keep it and then reward that keeping (Jeremiah 32:39–42). A covenant-keeping God and a covenant-keeping parent ensure that the children will be blessed: "But from everlasting to everlasting the Lord's love is with those who fear him, and his righteousness with their children's children—with those who keep his covenant and remember to obey his precepts" (Psalm 103:17–18).

Believing parent, see here the two sides of your calling: Be full of faith and be faithful. Let faith in the living God—in His covenant with you and your seed, in His promises for your children, in His faithfulness—fill your soul. Take God's Word as the only measure of faith. And then be very faithful: Take God's Word as the only measure of your life, especially with regard to your family. Be a parent such as God would have you to be. Study Abraham and his fatherhood as chosen of God, faithful to God, blessed of God—and find in him the type, the law, the promise of what your father roll can be.

PRAYER OF CONSECRATION

O God, have you truly taken me as well into this wonderful covenant, in which you are the God of the seed of your saints, and by which you make them the ministers of your grace to their children? Open my eyes, I pray, to see the full glory of your covenant, that my faith may know all that you have prepared for me to bestow, and may I do all that you have prepared for me to perform. May your covenant-keeping faithfulness be the life and the strength of my faith. And may this faith enable me to responsibly keep the covenant.

Teach me to realize fully what this parental faithfulness involves that you ask of me. I would make this the one object of my family life, to train my child to serve you. By my life, by my words, by my prayers, by gentleness and love, by authority and instruction, I would lead them in the way of the Lord. Be my helper, Lord.

Above all, help me to remember that you have appointed this parental training for the fulfillment of your purposes and that you have made provision for the grace to enable me to perform it. Let my faith envision your undertaking for me in all that I must do to raise my children to love you. I ask all this in the name of your Son. Amen.

Chapter 8

The Child's Surety

"Then Judah said to Israel his father, 'Send the boy along with me. . . . I myself will guarantee his safety; you can hold me personally responsible for him.'"

—Genesis 43:8–9

These are the words of Judah when he sought to persuade his father to send Benjamin with him to Egypt. By his pleadings before Joseph, it was evident that he realized what guardianship of the child meant and he was ready by any sacrifice to fulfill his duty: "I myself will guarantee his safety." And later he offered himself as a slave in his brother's place. In this he was the type not only of his own descendant, the great Surety of His people who gave himself in their stead, but also of every parent to whom God commits the care of a child amid the dangers of the journey through life. The language and conduct of Judah will teach us some helpful lessons.

Consider the *responsibility* of such a guardianship as was illustrated in Judah. He was thoroughly serious about the engagement he had undertaken. When the governor of Egypt had commanded that Benjamin should be kept as a slave, he at once came forward as a substitute. Not for a moment did he think of his own home and children or of Egyptian slavery and its hardships; everything gave way to the thought, *My father entrusted him to me, and I am surety for the lad.* With the most touching earnestness he pleaded to be accepted in the youth's stead: "Your servant guaranteed the boy's safety to my father. I said, 'If I do not bring him back to you, I will bear the blame before you, my father, all my life!' Now then, please let your servant remain here as my lord's slave in place of the boy, and let the boy return with his brothers" (Genesis 44:32–33).

Oh that Christian parents would realize, as Judah did, what it means to stand in that place for their child! How often—when our children are in danger because of the prince of this world, when the temptations of the flesh or the world threaten to make them prisoners and slaves, holding them back from ever reaching the Father's home—are we found careless or unwilling to sacrifice our ease and comfort in order to rescue them! How often the spiritual interests of the child are considered subordinate to our own worldly prospects or position or profit, and the solemn covenant is forgotten. How poorly we realize that it is only in a life of pure and wholehearted devotion, in which selfishness and worldly-mindedness are crucified and our life is lived for God, that we can truly train our children for heaven! When danger threatens, and our children appear to be growing up unconverted, we must bow at the foot of the throne until we see that our plea, "I myself will guarantee his safety," has touched the heart of the King and we have His word that they will be set free. Oh that the ruling principle of parental life and love might be: *Without the child I will not see my Father's face.*

Consider too the *encouragement* Judah's example gives. It sets before us the abundant reward faithful guardianship reaps. In pleading with the ruler of Egypt, Judah thought he was dealing with a stranger, a despot, an enemy. Little did he know that his pleadings were entering the ears of one who was his own—and Benjamin's—brother! He never dared to hope that it would exercise such a mighty influence, calling forth the wondrous revelation of the ruler—weeping on Benjamin's neck—"I am Joseph." What a wonderful picture of the power and reward of a guarantor's supplication!

And yet it is not more wonderful than the parent/guardian may expect. If we understood the sinfulness of human nature—even our children's, and the dangers surrounding them—we would fervently plead with the great King and Savior of the world for their salvation. It is then—no less than to Judah—that the blessing would come. It might be that at first, as it was with Judah, we have little concept of the tender relationship in which He stands to us—and to our children—as a Brother. As we plead for the child and show ourselves ready to make any sacrifice so that he may be saved, we will have our reward in the blessed revelation of what Jesus is to us and to our child. The blessing bestowed upon the pleading parent would be no less rich than to his charge.

Just as the man who brought his son with a demon to Jesus, the royal official who brought his son sick unto death, the woman who summoned Jesus when her daughter had died, the centurion who took responsibility for his sick servant, and the Syrophenician woman who sought Jesus when her daughter was possessed of an evil spirit—as well as the thousands of parents who have asked for help and wholeness for their children—we have proof that while they thought only of obtaining what their children needed, their prayers led to experiences of the power and love of the Savior, closer and more intimate fellowship with Him, and personal blessing they never found praying only for themselves. They saw Him with whom they were pleading descend, and say, "I am Jesus"; they saw Him embrace their loved one. Jesus was never so gloriously revealed as when they were pleading as parents and guardians for their children and those in their care.

And just as Judah learned that Joseph was the true guarantor of his family's earthly salvation, who through suffering had won the throne and their deliverance from famine and death, so parents will learn, the more they seek to fulfill their duties as those ultimately responsible for their children, that Jesus is their Guarantor of eternal salvation. He has not only undertaken their own personal salvation, He has secured the grace they need to fulfill their responsibilities to their offspring.

The vicarious principle on which redemption rests, "One for all," runs through the whole of its economy—especially as it appears in the family—that image of humanity as a whole. There the father is head, priest, and king—even as Christ—over his own house; the father is, in a limited sense but truly, guarantor for the child. As he, the surety on earth, draws nigh to the King and discovers in Him the great Surety, the revelation will give him new confidence and strength and joy in the work he has undertaken. In the light of the redemption and love and friendship of Jesus, the thought, *I must guarantee my child's safety*, will gain new clarity; devotion to the training of your children will become more earnest; the readiness to make any sacrifice to save them from the world will be more spontaneous; and the pleading of faith will hold more confidence and ultimate victory.

PRAYER OF CONSECRATION

Blessed Father, we fervently ask that you will open the eyes of all parents to see and know their holy calling. May they understand and realize that you are saying to them at the birth of each little one entrusted to their care: "In your hands is the full responsibility for this child's soul." May they realize, too, that with each child they have dedicated to you, they have accepted the solemn charge and answered, "You can hold me personally responsible for him."

O God, show us what the dangers are that surround our children. Give us the true spirit of a guarantor, the willingness to sacrifice all rather than be unfaithful to our charge. As we see the power of sin and the world threatening our children, may we plead for them as for our own life, even with the offer-

ing of our life, that our children may be saved from sin and Satan. As you see us interact day by day with our children, may this be the one desire born of our parental love: that they may be wholly yours. May this be our one aim in prayer and in training them.

And now, Lord Jesus, teach us as parents that as surely as you are the Guarantor of our salvation, we are the guarantors of our family's spiritual life. You who are the faithful One, make us faithful too. Amen.

CHAPTER 9

PROTECTING THE FAITH

"When she saw that he was a fine child, she hid him for three months."

—Exodus 2:2

"By faith Moses' parents hid him for three months after he was born, because they saw he was no ordinary child, and they were not afraid of the king's edict."

—Hebrews 11:23

The story of Moses leads us a step further in our study of the relationship between children and their parents' faith. It was faith that saw the fairness of the child; it was faith that feared not the king's wrath; it was faith that hid the child and saved his life. In each child born of believing parents, faith sees the same goodness, meets the same danger, and finds the same path of safety.

It was by faith Moses' parents *saw he was no ordinary child.* The natural love of a parent's heart doubtless made the child a beautiful one in the mother's eyes, but faith saw more than nature could. God opened the eyes, and there was the consciousness of something special, of a spiritual beauty that made their baby doubly precious. And so the eye of faith sees in each little one a divine goodness. Is this not a being created in God's image with the faint light of a divine glory, of an immortal life, shining from it? Here is an object of the great redemption, destined to be a partaker of the precious blood and the Holy Spirit of Jesus, to be the object of the joy of angels and God's everlasting love and pleasure—a child whose worth exceeds that of the whole world; a child that even in this life can be a brother of Jesus, a servant of God, a blessing for the immortal spirits of his fellowmen. Surely faith may call the newborn unspeakably fair, seeing him shining as a jewel in the crown of the Lamb—His joy and His glory. We have indeed a surer hope than ever Moses' parents had, and a brighter light in which the heavenly beauty of our offspring is reflected. *O Father, open the eyes of all your people, that in each little one you give them their faith may see an extraordinary child.*

It is faith that sees but *fears not* the danger. Pharaoh had commanded that the children of God's people should all be destroyed. He knew that if the children were cut off, the people would soon die out. There would be no need for the trouble and danger of war. The Prince of this world still pursues the same agenda. When parents take a decided stand for God, the world may despise or hate them; it soon learns that it is of little use to attempt to conquer them. But it knows a surer way. The spirit of the world claims possession of the children; if these are won, all are won. Too often Christian parents allow the world to prey upon their children. They grow up in comparative ignorance about the blessed Savior, are entrusted to the care of irreligious or worldly teachers, and are allowed to associate with those whose spirit and influence is altogether opposed to the ways of God.

In many Christian homes where at one time—when the children were young—religious training was all in earnest and consistent, the tone has changed, and as the children have grown older the influence and power of the family's faith is far less evident. Unfortunately, the church is often too unaware to warn against it. How little the church has realized, in fact, the importance of the parent/child relationship in the future of the church. To a large extent the education of the young has been left to the state, to the secular school, and to the spirit of the age, until the childlike heart has lost the simplicity and tenderness of which the Master spoke when He said, "Of such is the kingdom of heaven." Thus thousands of children are drowned in the mighty Nile of this world. Oh, that the eyes of God's people might be opened to the danger that threatens the church! It is not infidelity or superstition, *it is the spirit of worldliness in the homes of Christian families*, sacrificing the children to the ambitions of society, to the riches or the friendship of the world—that is the greatest danger of Christ's church. If every home once won for Christ were a training school for His service, we would find in this a secret of spiritual strength no less than all that ordinary preaching can accomplish.

It is faith that finds *the path of safety*. "By faith Moses' parents hid him for three months." They trusted God on behalf of their child, one of the children of His covenant. These simple words tell us our responsibility and what our faith must accomplish: Christian parent, hide your child. *But where?* you may say. In the safest refuge: the shadow of the Almighty, the strong arms of Jesus. From his birth, daily put your child there in faith, and let your soul be filled with the confidence that He has indeed covered him with His wings. Let the mighty rock of God's strength and the tender covering of His feathers be your child's ark while he is still unconscious of temptation or danger. With the first dawn of reason, may the clefts of the rock and the love of Jesus be the places of safety to which you guide the wandering feet. In the quiet of homelife, protect him from the excitements of the world without and from the influence of a people and culture that is only of this earth. In the refuge of the home, we have one of faith's highest duties—that of training and nurturing our children in the ways of the Lord and in His Word. And when the time comes that your child must have contact with the world, may there be a level of trust between you that keeps him on the narrow path and in the way of his training.

The *reward* of faith that Moses' parents knew will be ours. Not only was Moses saved, he also became the savior of his people. Your child, too, will not only be blessed but also be a blessing to others. Each child has a calling unique to his personality and talents. Let your faith, like that of Moses' mother, do its work; God himself will see to it that your labor is not in vain.

The education Moses' mother gave her son during the years of his childhood was such that all the years of training in Pharaoh's court could not obliterate it. His parents' faith bore fruit in his faith when he, at great cost, chose suffering with the people of God and was not afraid of the wrath of the king. Moses saw Him who is invisible. Train the child for God and His people, and when the time comes that he must go into the world, even into Pharaoh's court, he will be safe in the power of faith and of God's keeping.

God grant that the church also may become as Moses' mother, a faithful nurse of the children He entrusts to her care, hiding them and keeping them separate from the world and its influence. He will give a wonderful fulfillment of the promise wherever He finds the fulfillment of the duty: "Take this baby and nurse him for me, and I will pay you" (Exodus 2:9).

PRAYER OF CONSECRATION

Gracious God, with my whole heart I thank you for the teaching of your Word by which you prepare me to fulfill my holy calling as a parent. I thank you for the example of Moses' parents and pray that the grace that taught them in faith to save their child may be given to me also.

I acknowledge, Lord, that I do not sufficiently realize the value of my children or the danger to which they are exposed from the Prince and the spirit of this world. Lord, teach me fully to recognize the danger and yet never to fear the com-

mandment of the King. Open my eyes to see that in the light of heaven each child is a special child, entrusted to my keeping and training for your work and kingdom. Help me in the humility and watchfulness and boldness of faith to keep him sheltered, to hide him from the power of the world and of sin. May my own life be the life of faith, hid with Christ in God, that my child may know no other dwelling place.

Grant this also to all your people, Lord. Let your church awaken to know her place in this world and her calling to nurture the lambs in her care. Allow in the training of the children the mighty power of faith to be seen—the difference between those that fear you and those that do not. Oh, give us grace to rear our children for you. Amen.

CHAPTER 10

A LAMB FOR A HOUSE

"Tell the whole community of Israel that on the tenth day of this month each man is to take a lamb for his family, one for each household. . . . When the LORD goes through the land to strike down the Egyptians, he will see the blood on the top and sides of the doorframe and will pass over that doorway, and he will not permit the destroyer to enter your houses and strike you down."

—Exodus 12:3, 23

Of all the Old Testament sacrifices, there is none that gives a clearer or richer revelation of the person and work of our Lord than the Passover. However, the fact has often escaped observation that the whole institution of the Paschal Lamb aimed at deliverance not of individuals but of whole families in the houses of God's people. What else could be the meaning of the expression, "a lamb . . . for each *household*" or as in verse 21, "animals for your families" and "the blood on the top and sides of the *doorframe*"? As so it is expressly declared, "And when your children ask you, 'What does this ceremony mean to you?' tell them, 'It is the Passover sacrifice to the LORD, who passed over the houses of the Israelites in Egypt and spared our homes when he struck down the Egyptians'" (vv. 26–27).

Among the Egyptians it was the *firstborn* in every house who died, representing the family. In Israel it was the *firstborn* who through the blood was saved from the impending danger and consecrated for God. All this teaches that God lays down as a fundamental law in the Passover and the sprinkling of the blood that He deals with us not as individuals but as families. As He chose and blessed the seed of Abraham, so He blesses every household through the believing father who sprinkles the blood in obedience to His command. The lamb and its blood are the consecration of the dwellings and the family relationships of His people. In the hands of the father God places the destiny and the safety of the whole house.

Christ, our Passover, was slain for us. Even to the smallest particular, the foreshadowing of the Paschal feast was fulfilled in Him. Have we any warrant in God's Word for excluding this important feature and allowing the type to hold good in every aspect but this? Is the Old Testament feast to stand higher than the New, and the blood that was for the saving of the house now to be only for the individual? If this were true, the Christian parent might have every reason to envy the Jew; looking at the sprinkled blood, he enjoyed the privilege of knowing that he had done it to save not only himself but his whole household. Doesn't the Christian parent have the right to claim the blood for his children too? Christ the Lamb of God is still "a lamb for a house"! His blood may still be sprinkled upon the door that the destroyer may not enter. In the new covenant, and with the precious blood of Christ, the principle still holds: it is the believing father's right and duty to appropriate by faith the blood for his whole house. His faith has the divine warrant and will be rewarded with the divine blessing.

Let me strive from now on to live in this faith, fully realizing this privilege. As I think of the precious blood and seek to walk close to God, let me claim its cleansing power for my house as well as for myself. Let me be assured that my faith as a parent has power and secures a divine influence. Thank God that as a father I may transmit the grace and blessing of redemption to my children.

Not only my soul but also my house can daily be kept under the sprinkling and cleansing of the blood of Christ. And each time I enter my door, by the light of heaven I may see it sprinkled with the blood of the Lamb. Parents and children stand under the cover and protection of the blood: the Lord is our keeper.

Every year in Israel parents had to renew the sprinkling. *But the blood of the Lamb has been shed once for all.* I can each day renew the consecration of my house to the Lord in the assurance of faith; the blood saves me, and my children. In this faith I may confidently expect that the wondrous redemption of the blood will exercise its full and mighty influence until all our domestic life and its relationships are sanctified, our house belongs wholly to the Lord, and each child is consciously and by testimony one of His redeemed.

To this end I must notice carefully how God commanded the parents to teach these things to their children (Exodus 12:26; 13:14). "The grace of God that brings salvation *teaches* us." What is secured to the child in redemption must be made his own in free and personal appropriation. And this cannot be without his knowing it. The children were to be *taught* that they belonged to the redeemed people and to the redeeming God. The parent was to act not only as priest and thus, in a sense, as mediator, but also as prophet and teacher. As he had dealt with God for the children in the sprinkling of the blood, so he was to deal with God for the children in the instructions he gave them. Let me seek grace and wisdom to teach my children what the blood has done for them, to encourage them to know and love the God who accepted them before they knew Him!

One thing more is deserving of special note: Every year the believing Israelite was to sprinkle the doorposts with blood, so testifying that it was only in the blood that he and his house could stand before God; he was also to write upon these same blood-sprinkled doorposts the words of God's law (Deuteronomy 6:7–9). In all the going out and coming in of his children, these words were to meet their eyes. The freedom from Egypt's bondage and Egypt's curse was in effect a freedom to serve God. God would not only be trusted but also obeyed. It is unto obedience *and* the sprinkling of the blood of Christ that we have been chosen. The doorposts sprinkled with the blood and inscribed with the words of the law remind me of the blessed oneness of faith and obedience, liberty and service. I would in the joy of our redemption train and educate my children to know, love, and keep the commands of their God. Day by day, in faith and prayer, in teaching and living, I would seek to set before them the blessedness of a faith that freely accepts all that God gives with a surrender of all that He claims.

"A lamb for a house"—I pray that God's Holy Spirit will reveal in its full power all the truths that are contained in this blessed word. A father redeemed by the blood; his children through him and with him partaking of the provision; the father, God's minister to every year consecrate the house afresh; the father, God's witness and messenger to the children to teach them of this precious blood and of the God it represents; the blood-sprinkled doorposts inscribed with the words of God's law—such is God's wondrous provision for gaining full possession of His people.

PRAYER OF CONSECRATION

Blessed Lord Jesus, the Lamb of God, who takes away the sin of the world, the Son of God, whose blood cleanses from all sin, in humble faith I claim that blood for myself and for my children. May my own experience of its ever-cleansing power grow fuller and clearer. And may I by your Holy Spirit realize my right to claim it for my house.

Blessed Savior, may the power of your blood work in me so

mightily that my faith may in full assurance accept it for each of my children as a present blessing. May we, under the covering of the blood, know ourselves protected from the destroyer.

Gracious God, who has given this wondrous ordinance of a lamb for a house, I yield myself to you afresh as the minister of your covenant. Use me, my God, to save my children, to train them for you and you alone. I would have the doorposts not only sprinkled with the blood but also inscribed with your Law. I would have your service be the aim of my children. As you have chosen us unto obedience and application of your blood, may faith in that blood and surrender to your will be as the two doorposts between which we daily go in and out. The Lord make it so. Amen.

CHAPTER 11

THE FATHER—PRIEST AND PROPHET

"And when your children ask you, 'What does this ceremony mean to you?' then tell them, 'It is the Passover sacrifice to the LORD, who passed over the houses of the Israelites in Egypt and spared our homes when he struck down the Egyptians.' Then the people bowed down and worshiped."

—Exodus 12:26–27

The Passover sets the believing parent before us in a twofold aspect: first, as dealing with God on behalf of the children and calling down the blessing on them; then, as dealing with the children for God and seeking to lead them to Him. In the former capacity, he sprinkled the blood of the lamb upon his house, securing God's protection for the children. In the latter, he had to instruct his children, telling them what God had done and then seeking to lead them to a personal knowledge and acceptance of this God as their God. Those two parts of parental duty are closely and inseparably linked, the first being necessary as the root and origin of the latter. The parent's work as priest fits him for his work as prophet and teacher. The second is indispensable to the full appropriation of the blessing that the former has secured. It was after having sprinkled the blood for himself and for his child that the parent had to instruct the child in the meaning of the holy mystery. His own relationship with God and his experience of God's blessing were his own training to fit him for the training of his child. As we keep this in mind, we will recognize the beauty of that institution by which God has chosen and appointed the believing parent as the instructor of his children and realize its appropriateness as the best means of securing godly followers for the Lord.

It is the parent who has already experienced the salvation of God who is appointed to lead the child to know God. The knowledge of God is not only a matter of understanding; it is to love Him, live in Him, and experience the power of His presence and His blessing. It is obvious that anyone who would teach others to know God must be able to speak from personal experience, proving by the warmth of his love and devotion that he knows God and receives his life from Him.

When God instituted the family as the great instrument of transmitting His love, He arranged it so as to give it the highest possible efficacy. This consisted in revealing himself to each head of a family as the God of his salvation. In the other sacrifices in Israel, the priest sprinkled the blood in the holy places, but in the Passover there was this distinctive feature: *each father* sprinkled it *on his own house*. He thereby performed the act of faith by which the destroyer was kept from his house, and when he left Egypt and undertook the journey to Canaan, he could bear personal witness to God's faithfulness and the efficacy of the atoning blood of the lamb. He could speak as a living witness from personal experience. As a redeemed one, he could witness to redemption, he could tell others of the Redeemer-God.

Even now this is so: Personal experience of the power of the blood can alone equip a parent for speaking to his children about God. Looking back upon the time when personal deliverance from sin was experienced, looking to the God with whom a personal fellowship is maintained, and anticipating an eternal home prepared by the Father—this is what enables a parent to speak the truth in power. It is the parent who has himself experienced redemption who can best tell his child of the God of redemption, and who can act in accordance with the injunction, "On that day tell your son, 'I do this because of what the LORD did for me when I came out of Egypt'" (Exodus 13:8).

Just as parents in Israel had to renew the remembrance of that deliverance every year, so now it is the parent who lives in the fresh experience of the power of redemption who can with true conviction teach his children the truth of God. Furthermore, this parent has been *appointed by God* as the messenger of redemption to his child. This appointment gives an increased motivation for his work as model and teacher. He not only speaks of a salvation he has personally experienced, but in applying the blood upon his house by faith, he has saved his child from the destroying angel. What the child could not do for himself, the father has done for him. The child has been made partaker of the blessing of that blood covering on the home, even though in growing up he must come personally to accept what has been secured and sealed for him.

What a great advantage this gives the believing parent's efforts, when he can look upon his child in the light of that great transaction between God and himself. What confidence it inspires for urging the child to submit to Christ. He speaks to him not as a stranger to the covenant of grace but as a child of the covenant. He points him to a God who has dealt with him from infancy by way of the covenant entered into between God and the parent and sealed in the application of the blood. He further encourages the child to submit himself to the God whom the family embraces.

The covenant also gives the parent power in pleading with God on behalf of the child. He reminds Him of the blood and the oath of the covenant and claims for his child the blessings of redemption. Next to his own personal experience of salvation, this consciousness of what as a believing parent he has been allowed to do—bringing his seed into covenant with him—qualifies him to be the minister of God's grace to his child.

But there is another thought that brings out even more clearly the adaptation of the family constitution for the working out of God's purposes—namely, that *it is grounded in the natural relationship*, sanctifying its affections, and adopting them into the service of redemption. It is not merely a redeemed man saying to his fellowman, "Come and see what God has done for me." Nor is it a redeemed man saying to some child to whom he sustains a certain official relationship and on whose behalf he has performed an act of atonement, "Come and let me lead you to your God." Rather, *it is a father with his own child.* In nature they are one, united by the closest of ties. The child has his life from the father; the father looks upon him as part of himself—of his flesh and of his bones; he loves and cherishes him. This love seeks even in nature the happiness of the child, and can often make wondrous sacrifices to attain it. It is this love that God lays hold of in the parental covenant, purifying it to be the minister and vehicle of His grace.

With a parent's love comes a parent's influence. The weakness of the child renders him dependent to a great degree upon the parent's will. The character of a child is formed and molded by impressions; continual communion with the parent can render these impressions deep and permanent. The child's love for a parent rises to meet the parent's love, and the spirit of the parent can be in a sense breathed into the child. Of all this God's grace seeks to avail itself. And while it is the sole prerogative of the Holy Spirit to renew the soul and make one a child of God, there is nevertheless a need for the means and instruments through which His gracious workings are prepared and applied, confirmed and established. Of all these instruments, there is none more wondrously devised or more beautifully adapted to its object than godly parentage. A parent who is made partaker of God's love and grace himself, who is accepted and blessed with the promises of the covenant and the Spirit, and who through the power of consecrated devotion makes all the influences and relationships of family life the means of gaining his child for God—this is surely one of the most brilliant displays of God's grace on earth.

Prayer of Consecration

O God, I come to you again with the earnest prayer for your teaching. You have said, "I will be the God of all the families of Israel." Open my eyes to see clearly and my heart to feel deeply what your purpose is in this.

Since sin entered and ruined our nature, you would early take possession of the little ones for yourself. You seek to secure parents with all their love and influence to be your ministers. You enter into covenant with them, giving them the right to claim the blood of the covenant for their children and in that blood the promise, "a God to you and to your seed." And then you send them, redeemed and having claimed and accepted redemption for their children, to use their influence for you and to win and train their children for your love and service.

Lord God, open the eyes of the parents of your church to their calling that they may honor you as the God of their families. And, Lord, bless my own house! Give me grace, as one of your redeemed ones, to train my children for you. May the joy of a personal experience of redemption and the love of the blessed Redeemer warm my heart, inspire my words, and light my life to testify of you and to train my children for you alone. Amen.

CHAPTER 12

SANCTIFY THE FIRSTBORN

"The LORD said to Moses, 'Consecrate to me every firstborn male. The first offspring of every womb among the Israelites belongs to me, whether man or animal. Redeem with a lamb every firstborn donkey, but if you do not redeem it, break its neck. Redeem every firstborn among your sons. In days to come, when your son asks you, "What does this mean?" say to him, "With a mighty hand the LORD brought us out of Egypt, out of the land of slavery. When Pharaoh stubbornly refused to let us go, the LORD killed every firstborn in Egypt, both man and animal. This is why I sacrifice to the LORD the first male offspring of every womb and redeem each of my firstborn sons."'"

—Exodus 13:1–2, 13–15

We see in the words so often repeated by the Lord in sending Moses to Pharaoh, "Let my people go that they may serve me," how service is the aim of redemption. God frees His people from the bondage of Egypt in order to translate them into the liberty of His service—the willing, loving, free service of a redeemed people. The deeper God's people enter into the spirit of redemption, the deeper will be their insight into the blessed unity of liberty and service. There is no true service of God without freedom, no true freedom without service.

We see in the Passover the permanent place the whole family

takes in redemption. No less than their parents, the children are redeemed to serve; all their training is for the service of God. When Pharaoh said to Moses after the plague, "Go, worship the LORD your God. . . . But just who will be going?" the answer was plain, "We will go with our young and old, with our sons and daughters." It was on this point that the negotiations were broken off. It was the going of the children that the king would not consent to: "The LORD be with you—if I let you go, along with your women and children! Clearly you are bent on evil" (Exodus 10: 8–10).

Later on Pharaoh still wanted to keep the property. He felt that this at least must be conceded: "Go, worship the LORD. Even your women and children may go with you; only leave your flocks and herds behind" (v. 24). It is the future of the nation that is to be secured for God; a people that will serve God must in the first place see to their little ones.

After the people had left Egypt, the very first command God gave to Moses was in regard to the firstborn, who were to be separated and sanctified for Him. In each family the firstborn son was counted the chief and the best. The father's attitude toward him is expressed in these words of Jacob concerning Reuben: "You are my firstborn, my might, and the beginning of my strength."

His was the birthright and the place of honor in the family. He was the representative and head of all the children. God looked upon Israel as His firstborn among the nations. Because Egypt oppressed her and would not let her go, God slew Egypt's firstborn. And then in commemoration of this and as a pledge of God's claim on all the children and the whole people, every firstborn belonged to God and was set apart as His property.

And what was the object? Service unto Him. This comes out distinctly in the exchange that was made when the tribe of Levi was taken instead of the firstborn: "After you have purified the Levites and presented them as a wave offering, they are to come to do their work at the Tent of Meeting. They are the Israelites who are to be given wholly to me. I have taken them as my own in place of the firstborn, the first male offspring from every Israelite woman. Every firstborn male in Israel, whether man or animal, is mine. When I struck down all the firstborn in Egypt, I set them apart for myself" (Numbers 8:15–17). And in the redemption money, which had to be paid at the birth of each firstborn for his release, the parents had the unceasing reminder that he belonged to God and His service and was represented in the Levites.

The principle involved in this is one of deep importance. *God claims our best for His own direct and immediate service.* The whole people, old and young, were to serve Him; but the firstborn were to be entirely set apart for the special maintenance of that service, not only by the part they took in the worship but also by instructing the people in the Law of their God. Let us seek to take full advantage of the lessons the Christian church has to learn from this.

In Israel, all the firstborn and, as their representatives, all the children of Levi—a twelfth of the whole nation—were exclusively claimed by God to be continually at His disposal in the service of His house. And in Israel that service consisted solely in the maintenance of what existed—nothing had to be done for the extension of the kingdom or the propagation of the knowledge of God among the heathen. The Christian church now must see to it that she maintains her hold on what she once occupied; her calling in her redemption from sin is distinctly and essentially aggressive, to teach all the nations and seek the extension of the kingdom throughout the whole world. The question follows: If Israel had to set apart one-twelfth of its children for the work of God, what portion should the Christian church devote to the work committed to her? What portion has she devoted?

The sad truth is, there is hardly a missionary agency engaged in teaching and rescuing the lost that has not complained of the lack of laborers. The call goes out louder every year that many doors to the millions of heathen are open wide, and yet how few are the laborers. Why is this? Is it because Christian parents do not, as a rule, educate their children under the conviction that they belong to the Lord and to His service? Do they train them to look upon this as their highest privilege, to be found worthy to bear the name of Christ among the lost?

Let us think a moment what would be thought of the loyalty of Englishmen to their queen if it were found difficult to find men to form her bodyguard or accept appointments in her service. Or what of the enthusiasm of an army where the general could not obtain sufficient numbers of volunteers for a post of danger and honor? And Jesus Christ, our King, who came to seek and save the lost, has said that these are His guard of honor, having His richest rewards, who forsake all for His and the gospel's sake. And yet while in many professions there are complaints of more applicants than openings, the Master must wait and His work must suffer because His people do not understand that they and their children have been redeemed to serve Him who gave himself for them.

What is the cure for this complacency? And what can we do, each in our family and community, to remedy it? We can devote every child under our care to God and His service. Let us not pray that our children may be saved without thinking of offering them as well to serve. Let us stop encouraging honorable and lucrative professions for our children, making the truth that they can serve God in any calling an excuse for neglecting special Christian service. Let us lay each child upon the altar, especially our firstborn, and seek this one thing: that they may become worthy and fit to be set apart for the service of the King.

Let the church learn as part of her preaching of redemption to lift aloud her voice, and cry, "You are redeemed for service, you and your children." The reason so many parents who have prayed for the salvation of their child have been disappointed is that the prayer was a selfish one; it was based on the desire to see the child happy and safe, and their own reputation intact, giving little thought to the glory of God or of consecration to His service. When God established His covenant with Abraham and gave him Isaac, His desire was to have Isaac at His disposal as a channel of blessing to the world. When God rewarded the faith of Moses' parents, He was looking for a servant through whom He could save Israel. When God redeemed Israel's firstborn on the night of the Passover, it was to have them for himself. God wants your children for His blessed service of love and liberty. He gave His firstborn, His only-begotten Son, for you and your children; can anything be too precious to offer Him? Don't entertain thoughts that the demand is hard or the sacrifice great. Know that for yourself, as for your children, it is the path of honor and blessing. Let your example teach the church that there are those who, because they love their children intensely, know nothing better for them than to yield them completely to the will and the work of God.

PRAYER OF CONSECRATION

O Lord, you are a great and a glorious God, and your kingdom rules over all. You alone are worthy to be praised; you alone have the right to the love and worship and service of all your creatures. In heaven above and on earth below, blessed are your servants who stand around your throne and do your will.

Lord, we bless you that you ask for and accept our children for your service. We acknowledge this claim; let them be used for your service and glory. Make them willing and happy to give themselves over to the work of your kingdom.

O God, teach us to feel deeply that you have need of them. For the building up of your temple, in the struggle of your kingdom with the powers of darkness, in the gathering of your people from the millions of lost, you have need of our children. We give them to you. We will train them for you. We will wait in prayer and faith, and we beseech you to inspire them with a holy enthusiasm for the kingdom and its conquests. We beseech you to fill them and us with love to Jesus and love to souls that they may serve you as your Son did, giving their lives to save others.

You who have redeemed us and our children by the blood of the Lamb, let our firstborn—let all our children—be holy unto the Lord. Amen.

CHAPTER 13

THE SABBATH AND CHILDREN

"Remember the Sabbath day by keeping it holy. Six days you shall labor and do all your work, but the seventh day is a Sabbath to the LORD your God. On it you shall not do any work, neither you, nor your son or daughter, nor your manservant or maidservant, nor your animals, nor the alien within your gates."

—Exodus 20:8–10

Among the most precious blessings that a child from a godly home can take with him into the world is the habit of reverent observance of the Sabbath. The separation from evil company, leading him to God's house, the calm and thoughtful quiet it sometimes brings over his spirit will, even if he is still a stranger to grace, be a safeguard and a help, a schoolmaster to bring him to Christ. If he is a Christian, it will be one of his greatest aids in the growth and strengthening of the life of faith. The training is a part of a parent's duty that needs to be studied in earnest prayer and for the performance of which much wisdom and grace are needed. The Lord, who has given the command, will not withhold the grace.

Note in the words of the fourth commandment how particularly the children are remembered. It is to parents the command is given; it is in the keeping holy of the day by their children, as well as by themselves, that their obedience is to be manifested. "... you, nor your son or daughter, nor your manservant or maidservant": it is not so much as a private or a national ordinance, but as a family one that the Sabbath was first appointed. Just as the terms of the covenant, "a God to you and to your seed," the words suggest the two thoughts that it is first the parent, and then the child through the parent, with whom God is dealing. The parent must first learn to keep the Sabbath day holy himself, and then train his child to keep it holy too.

The parent's obedience of this command precedes the training of the child to do so. Here is the principle that lies at the root of all true education: What I wish to develop in my child I must first practice myself. Example is more than precept, more than teaching; what I am and do is more important than what I tell my child to be or do. The question is often asked how we can teach our children to revere and love the Sabbath, and many answers of great value have been given. But we cannot emphasize too much the truth that the first requirement is that the parents reverently and habitually keep the day holy themselves. It is as they serve God in the beauty of holiness, and the spirit of holiness breathes on them in the services of the Sabbath, that the day will become not simply one of strict observance, but of joyful worship, quickened devotion, and loving fellowship with God. As the Sabbath becomes a delight, the first condition will be fulfilled for teaching their children to love it.

Let Christian parents note: God means the Sabbath to be to your child what it is to your own experience, a day that you look forward to and rejoice in. Let us study its wonderful significance and rich blessing.

Look upon the Sabbath as the day of *rest*, of entering into God's rest. God's rest is in a finished work; by faith in that work we enter into the same repose, the calm, the peace that passes all understanding (Genesis 2:2–3; Hebrews 4:3–10).

Look upon the day as a *holy* day, the day God has given as a token and pledge that He who is holy makes us holy too (Exodus 31:13; Ezekiel 20:12). It is in fellowship with God that we are made holy; let His presence, His love, His joy, be the mark as well as the fruit of keeping it holy.

Look upon it as a day of *blessing* (Genesis 2:3). Sin robbed mankind of this blessing. In the resurrection of Christ the finished work of creation was restored, perfected in a higher sense. Under the leading of the Holy Spirit, the first day of the week, the day of the Lord Jesus, the Sabbath of the new life, took the place of the Sabbath of death, when the Lord of the Sabbath was in the tomb. The Sabbath of creation, rendered void by the Fall and the Law, is now glorified in the Sabbath of redemption. And all the blessings of the living Christ—His finished work and resurrection power and eternal rest and the Holy Spirit, who descended from heaven on this new Sabbath—are to be made ours by this day. Let it be to us a day of blessing in the fellowship of the Father's love and the Son's grace through the Holy Spirit. In so doing we will have taken the first and the surest step for its being a blessing and a joy to our sons and daughters.

So we see that it is not enough that the parent keep the Sabbath day holy; the Lord lays on him the responsibility to secure the child's doing so as well. As a parent he is responsible for his child's keeping the Sabbath and must make it a matter of distinct effort and prayer. The training of children to do so is a sacred obligation and requires, on account of its difficulty, the sacrifice of personal enjoyment, the exercise of thought and wisdom, patient faith, and love.

In seeking to do this, there are two dangers to be avoided. In human nature we find that there are two principles implanted in our hearts to guide us in action: pleasure and duty. The former leads us to seek what is agreeable and for our own interest and is one of the most powerful motives in all our conduct. When our pleasure, however, is at variance with the interests of others or the will of God, the sense of duty comes forward to restrain and regulate the desire for pleasure. The reward of obedience to duty is that in the course of time it is no longer a check to pleasure but becomes itself the highest pleasure. The art of education consists in so bringing pleasure and duty into harmony that without the sacrifice of either both may be attained.

In training the child to keep the Sabbath day, there is a danger of putting either of these principles too exclusively in the forefront. With our Puritan and covenant-keeping ancestors, duty was the only principle urged, and the only sanction sought for keeping the Sabbath was the Law. In our day, we are in danger of the opposite extreme. To make the Sabbath interesting to the children, to make them happy in it—if possible to make them love it as a day of enjoyment—is so exclusively the object of attention that the thought of obligation is almost lost sight of. The idea is unconsciously instilled that the day is to be hallowed and loved only as far as it is made interesting and pleasant. Let parents seek grace from Him who, as divine wisdom teaches, guides us in paths of righteousness, to keep us from the right-hand as well as the left-hand error.

Do not hesitate to speak of God's command and of our duty. God trained Israel as He would a child in the life of the Law. Education consists, in its first stages, more in training to right habits than inculcating principles—these come later. In connection with the Lord's day, do be not afraid of the element of self-denial and self-control that the thought of obedience to God's will and to yours brings over a child's spirit. They are part of the foundation of noble character. Tranquility of mind and serenity of spirit are invaluable blessings; the quiet of the Sabbath helps to foster them. Holiness is much more than separation; it is a positive fellowship and enjoyment of God. But it begins with separation: the putting away of weekday toys and books and companions, the setting apart of the day from other days. Even the smaller issues are, under wise guidance, a preparation for the keeping of the day later on.

On the other hand, exercise a wise and loving thoughtfulness as to the ways in which the day can be made a happy one. In the illustrated lessons to the younger ones, in the careful selection of suitable and interesting reading material for the older ones, in the singing of psalms and hymns and spiritual songs, in the forethought with which possible breaking of the Sabbath is averted, in the tone of glad and loving reverence with which the day is spoken of and spent, and in personal Bible study and prayer, the believing parent will find the means of leading the child on to call the Sabbath a delight, the holy of the Lord, and to inherit the blessing promised to those who do so.

Dear Christian parents, the thought of how we ought to train our children to love the Sabbath reminds us of our shortcomings. But let not this discourage us. We have God, the God of the Sabbath, who gave the day as a token of the covenant He has with us and with our children to sanctify us. We have Him to teach us how to sanctify His day. Let us look to Him to give grace to feel and show that the Lord's day is the happiest day of the week. In the divided life of the ordinary worldly Christian it cannot be so. God's commandments cannot be obeyed without a wholehearted surrender to live for Him alone, without a life under the full power of His Holy Spirit. But if God is our chief joy, the desire after His service and love our highest aim, He himself will sanctify our Sabbaths, our hearts, our homes, our children, by His holy presence. And our Sabbaths will be but a part of a life wholly dedicated to the Lord.

PRAYER OF CONSECRATION

Most Holy God, I do thank you for the precious gift of the holy Sabbath day and the wonderful blessings of which it is the promise. I thank you above all for the redemption of the Sabbath, in the death of Jesus from the power of sin and its restoration to us in the power and the joy of His risen life. Grant that each succeeding Sabbath may lead me deeper into your rest, the rest of God in Christ, and so into the fellowship of your holiness and your blessedness. May a daily life that seeks its only joy in Christ, wholly yielded to the Spirit, prepare me for keeping the day holy.

Blessed Father, I especially ask for grace to train my children to love and hallow your day. I know that nothing but the joy of your presence in my own life can fit me for it. Give me this. And then give me the wisdom, as your servant, to bring to them the sense of your holy will and your loving-kindness, in claiming the day for yourself, and then in giving it to them as your own day, that the fear of grieving you and the joy of pleasing you may each find due place in their hearts. So may the command and the promise, the duty and the pleasure, be as one to them, and their delight in your day indeed meet the promised reward, "Then will you delight yourself in the Lord." Amen.

CHAPTER 14

THE CHILDREN'S COMMANDMENT

"Honor your father and your mother, so that you may live long in the land the LORD *your God is giving you."*
—Exodus 20: 12

"Children, obey your parents in the Lord, for this is right."
—Ephesians 6:1

"Children, obey your parents in everything, for this pleases the Lord."
—Colossians 3:20

The first four commandments have reference to God, the last five to our neighbor. In between stands the fifth. It is linked to the first four because to the young child the parent represents God; from him the child must learn to trust and obey God. And this command is the transition to the last five because the family is the foundation of society, and there the first experience comes of all the greater duties and difficulties with humankind at large. As the training school for all our relationships with God and people, this commandment lies at the foundation of all divine and human law, of all our worship of God and all our dealings with others.

Of the ten, the fifth is especially the "children's commandment." And on that account it is the parents' commandment also. A wise ruler makes good subjects, a firm commander makes faithful soldiers; it is on the parents' character that the children's fulfillment of this precept will depend. And so we will consider what parents must be if they are to succeed in training their children to honor them.

The sentiment of honor, or reverence, is one of the noblest and purest of which our nature is capable. The power to perceive what is worthy of honor, the willingness to acknowledge it, the unselfishness that feels it not as a degradation but a pleasure to render it—all this is itself honorable and ennobling; nothing brings more honor than giving honor to others. This disposition ought to be cultivated very carefully in the child as an important part of his education. It is one of the chief elements of a noble character and preparation for rendering to God the honor due Him.

If the teaching of Scripture to honor God, to honor all men, to honor the widows, to give honor to whom honor is due is to be obeyed by our children, they must be prepared for it by learning first to honor their parents. If they are in later life to do what is so difficult—to honor all men, by recognizing even in the degraded and the lost the worth that belongs to them who are created in the image of God—they must be carefully prepared for it in the home school of family life. This is not only to secure a happy home and place the relationship of parent and child on a right footing, but also to fit the child for all his future relationships to God and his fellowmen and to lay in him one of the foundation-stones of a noble character and a holy life. God has placed this commandment the first of those on the second table. Parents may well study how they can train their children to fulfill it.

The child must honor the parent by obedience. "Obey your parents" is the New Testament version of "Honor your father and your mother." The importance of the word *obedience* is more than the mind can grasp. God created man with the wonderful liberty of free will that he might obey Him by choice. Obedience to God was to lead to the enjoyment of God. By disobedience, sin entered; in obedience—the twofold obedience of Christ and to Christ (Hebrews 5:8–9)—salvation comes. And on the parent the sacred charge is laid of training the child to obey, teaching him to link all the memories of happiness and love in homelife with obedience, working the principle into the very mind and heart—not so much by instruction or reasoning as by training and securing the habit of obedience. The child is to be taught to honor the parent. The will of the child, no less than his mind and affections, is given into the parent's hands to mold and to guide. It is in yielding his will to the will of the parent that the child acquires that mastery over it and over himself, which will afterward be his strength and safety, making him a fit instrument for doing God's will. Man was created free that he might obey; obedience is the path to liberty.

On this point parents often err; they often say that to develop the will of the child the will must be left free and the child left to decide for himself. They forget that the will of the child is not free: passion and prejudice, selfishness and ignorance, all seek to influence the child in the wrong direction. The superior judgment, the calmer deliberation, the fuller experience of the parent are to decide for the child whose will has been entrusted to his care.

You may ask, are we not in danger of repressing the healthy development of a child's moral powers by thus demanding implicit submission to our will? By no means. The true liberty of the will consists in our being master of it and so our own masters. Train a child to master his will in giving it up to his parents' command, and he acquires the mastery to use it when he is free. Yielding to a parent's control is the path to self-control; and self-control alone is liberty. The child who is taught by a wise parent to honor and accept his superior wisdom will acquire, as he gives up his own way, the power over his will in a measure never possible to one who is taught that he need do nothing unless the parent has first convinced him of the propriety of the act and obtained his consent. The New Testament says very distinctly, "Children, obey your parents in the Lord: for *this is right*." Not because the child approves or agrees, but because the command is given by a parent—this is the reason why it must be obeyed.

In his attitude and conduct the child must be trained to honor the parent. Familiarity breeds contempt; in language and carriage and conduct, parents often tolerate an easygoing familiarity, mistakenly termed *love* or kindness, that destroys those sentiments of respect and reverence in which true love has its strength and its real happiness. Manners are more important than many think; the neglect of good manners not only reveals a lack in the disposition of those sentiments of respect and courtesy but it also affects the attitude and fosters the selfishness and indifference that cares little for others' feelings. Some say that next to religion and virtue, manners are the most important thing in education—more so even than learning. Let parents remember that in taking trouble to train their children to show them due honor and respect, even in apparently insignificant things, they are forming habits and principles in them that will afterward repay all their efforts. "Him that honors me, I will honor" is God's principle that has its reflection in the earthly life as well as the spiritual.

And it is the parent who is to cultivate and develop this sentiment in the child. The young child is guided not by reflection or argument but by feeling and affection. He cannot yet realize and honor the unseen God. He cannot yet honor all people, the mean and unworthy, for the unseen worth of their creation in God's image. The child can only honor what he sees to be "worthy of honor." And this is the parent's high calling: always so to speak and act, so to live in the child's presence, that honor may be spontaneously and unconsciously rendered. This can be only where, in quiet self-recollection and self-control, the parent lives in the fear of God and in His presence and walks worthy of this

107

calling, as one who has been placed at the head of a family to be not only its prophet and priest but also its king. Yes, a king receives honor. Let the parent reign as a king, ruling in love and the fear of God, and honor will be given him.

Above all, let parents remember that honor comes from God. Let them honor Him in the eyes of their children, and He will honor them there too. From parents who in everything seek to honor God, children will learn to honor God and them together. The parent who teaches his child to obey the fifth commandment has guided his feet into the way of all God's commandments. A child's first virtue is honoring and obeying his parents.

PRAYER OF CONSECRATION

O my God, I come again to you with the request that you would open my eyes and make me realize fully the parent's holy calling to train his child for all that you would have him be. I ask of you to especially reveal to me in your own light the full importance of the fifth commandment that I may teach my child to fulfill it according to your will.

Fill my own soul, I pray, with such honor and reverence for your holy majesty that both my child and I may learn what honor is. Teach me to claim honor from my child with the aim of leading him to honor you above all. May honoring his parents and honoring his God work in him the spirit of humility, which gladly renders to all what is due.

Lord, I look to you for grace to secure the keeping of this "children's commandment" in my home. Grant that I may always live worthy of all honor. And may the holy power to train young souls to keep your commandments, to honor and serve you, be the fruit of your own Spirit's work in me. I ask it, my God, in Jesus' name. Amen.

CHAPTER 15

PARENTAL INSTRUCTION

"These are the commands, decrees and laws the LORD your God directed me to teach you to observe in the land that you are crossing the Jordan to possess, so that you, your children and their children after them may fear the LORD your God as long as you live by keeping all his decrees and commands that I give you, and so that you may enjoy long life. Love the LORD your God with all your heart and with all your soul and with all your strength. These commandments that I give you today are to be upon your hearts. Impress them on your children. Talk about them when you sit at home and when you walk along the road, when you lie down and when you get up."
—Deuteronomy 6:1–2, 5–7

"You, your children and their children"—with these words in the second verse, Moses gave expression to the truth that God gave His commandments not merely to the individual or to a single generation, but to all people throughout history. Each one who received the commandments of God was to strive not only to keep them himself but to also hold himself responsible for their maintenance among his children. "These commandments that I give you today . . . impress them on your children. Talk about them when you sit at home and when you walk along the road, when you lie down and when you get up." Further down, in verses 20 and 21, is brought out the responsibility of expounding to the children the basis for the wondrous relationship in which God's people stood to Him. They had been favored with the divine Law, even the mercy and faithfulness of God who had redeemed them from the land of Egypt. All this concentrated in the one important and blessed truth that the fear and faith of God must be the basis for a family's beliefs. The greatest means for maintaining and extending this fear and faith of God among His people is the consistent performance of parental duty that His service and blessing might descend from son to son.

Parental instruction must come *from the heart*. We all know how little is learned from a spiritless or uninterested teacher. It is only the heart that gains the heart, the loving warmth of care and affection that can awaken corresponding emotions in the pupil. God would take all the influence of parental love to gain access for His words and will into the minds and hearts of the children of His people. He says, "You shall love the Lord your God with all your heart . . . and these commandments . . . are to be upon your hearts. Impress them on your children."

How easy and blessed the work, so often sighed over, if not neglected completely, to those who listen to God's guidance. As is your duty, love the Lord your God with all your heart. If you love Him, love His words; let them live in your heart, have a place in your affections. And if the heart is filled with God's love and God's words, how easy it will be to have them in your mouth, too, and to teach them to your children. Let holy love to God and His words mingle with your fond and tender love to your little ones, and it will be a joyous work to win the beloved on earth to the beloved Father in heaven.

When the work of instructing children threatens to become a burden or a wearisome task, you may be sure it is a sign of something wrong within: love toward God is waning or delight in His Word is fading. As you seek for fresh enthusiasm to perform your work hopefully and joyfully, you only have to turn to the words that reveal the secret of a godly education. There is an unspeakable blessing in the wisdom that has so inseparably connected the heart's secret love with the mouth's spoken words: "You shall love the Lord your God with all your heart . . . and these commandments . . . are to be upon your hearts. Impress them on your children." The divinely appointed ministry and means for the salvation of our children is parental love elevated and strengthened by the love of God, *guided* and *inspired* by His own Holy Word.

Parental instruction must be diligent and serious. But no cold declaration of God's will, no mere intellectual knowledge will be adequate. The godly parent must consider how he can best access the heart of his particular child, how he can best gain both the child's understanding and affections, looking for the best opportunities for keeping his interest, and through careful preparation by prayer and study present God's love and redemption in words the child can grasp and understand. He strives to make his own life an attractive example of what he has taught. There is nothing that drives home the word of instruction as powerfully as a consistent and holy life. Above all, the parent seeks to teach by waiting for the Holy Spirit, who alone can make the Word as sharp as a two-edged sword. With His aid the parent may experience the truth of Ecclesiastes 12:11: "The words of the wise are like goads, their collected sayings like firmly embedded nails—given by one Shepherd." God's promise is sure: from earnest, painstaking, and prayerful effort the blessing of the Spirit will not be withheld.

And to this end the parental instruction must be *persevering and continuous*: "Talk about them when you sit at home and when you walk along the road, when you lie down and when you get up." The entrance of divine truth into the mind and heart, the formation of habits and the training of character— these are not attained by sudden and isolated efforts, but by regular and unceasing repetition. This is the law of all growth in nature, and God uses the same law in the kingdom of grace.

This is the principle that is so beautifully applied by Moses to parental duty. The instruction he imposed was not to be by means of set times and stated formal lectures; the whole life with all its duties was to be interwoven with the lessons of God's presence and service. With a heart full of God's love and God's Word, the ordinary occupations of daily life were not to be hindrances but helps in leading young hearts to God.

The children were taught that faith and devotion were not matters that could be accomplished in one day, in the moments of morning or evening prayers, but by a continual and spontaneous speaking out of the heart, proving that God's presence and love were a reality and a delight. Sitting in the home or walking by the way, now in quiet rest, now in the labors and duties of the day, with the Bible or with books of God's glory in nature at hand—all equally afforded opportunity for recognizing the goodness of the ever-present One. The whole day and the whole life was occasion for uninterrupted fellowship with the Holy One and for pointing the little ones to the Father in heaven. And lest the objection should be made that all the speaking would tire and alienate—an objection often made against mere talk while heart and life deny the reality—we point once more to the source and secret of all: loving the Lord your God with all your heart. And keeping His words in your heart, that you may teach them to your children. May each of you receive wisdom from on high and be guided by divine love to know when and how to speak—how to influence your children's hearts with the flame of your own zeal, finding a willing and loving ear and not a weary one.

PRAYER OF CONSECRATION

O Lord, I thank you for each new reminder of the value that my relation to my children has in your sight, and of your call to me as a parent to carry out your purposes. May each thought of loving and serving you be connected with your

Word, "You and your children . . ."; and may each act of faith claim for my child all I seek for myself.

Blessed God, give me wisdom and grace to be a teacher of my children as you would have me be. You have chosen no other to take a parent's place; you have appointed him the first and best teacher. Lord, teach me, with all parents, to learn the lessons that you see we need to fit us for our work.

Fill our hearts with your love and your Word. Love knows no sacrifice, counts nothing a burden; love does not rest until it has triumphed. Oh, fill us with your love; shed it abroad in our hearts by the Holy Spirit. And fill us with your Word, that teaching our children will be the spontaneous overflow of our hearts. Make us diligent and wise to do our work well. Sharpen your words to go deep into our children's hearts. And make us to persevere each day, walking in your love and presence. Make our whole life an influence, educating our children for you.

Father, help us for Jesus' sake. Amen.

CHAPTER 16

A CONSECRATED HOME

"But if serving the LORD seems undesirable to you, then choose
for yourselves this day whom you will serve, whether the gods
your forefathers served beyond the River, or the gods of the Am-
orites, in whose land you are living. But as for me and my
household, we will serve the LORD."

—Joshua 24:15

In God's dealings with Noah and Abraham, and with Israel
in the Passover and at Mount Sinai, we see repeatedly the mention of father and children as these relate to His commands and
promises. "You *and* your house," "you *and* your seed," "you *and*
your children," "you *and* your son." Such is always the language
of the covenant God. In the words of Joshua we have the response from earth, "As for me *and* my household. . . ." The principle of divine dealing is accepted: the parent boldly vouches for
his family as well as for himself; the covenant engagement of the
Father in heaven is met by the covenant obligation of the father
on earth. Here Joshua is to us the model of a godly parent, and
in him we can see what parental guidance in the faith ought to
be.

Let it be a *personal* faith. "But as *for me* and my household . . ."—he began with himself. We cannot emphasize too
strongly the truth that for a godly education the first and the

90

most essential prerequisite is personal consecration. It is good to reflect on our responsibility, to study our duties and the best way of fulfilling them, to speak with our children and to pray continually for them—but all these may be called accessories. The first and most important action on the part of the parent is to maintain a life devoted to God and His service. It is this commitment that creates the spiritual atmosphere for the children.

There must be no hesitation or halfheartedness in the confession of our devotion to God's service. As often as the prayer for God's blessing on the children comes up, it must be in the spirit of David: "You, Lord God, know *your servant*. Now let it please you to bless the house of *your servant*." With God and men, in the home and out of it, it must be a settled thing in the heart of a parent: "But as for me . . . [I] will serve the LORD."

But let yours be without question a *family* faith. Take a stand for all who belong to you: "But as for me *and my household, we* will serve the LORD." There are committed parents who do not understand that this is their duty and their privilege. They don't know what God has placed in their power. They imagine they are honoring God by thinking that the faith of their children is dependent upon God's will apart from their instrumentality. They are so occupied, either with the engagements of their calling in this life, or even with Christian work, that they cannot find the time for speaking out and acting out the bold statement: "As for me and my household, *we will* serve the LORD." Or perhaps the father leaves the Christian upbringing of the children to the care of the mother, while the mother thinks that the father, as head of the house, is responsible. They hesitate or neglect to come to a clear and definite understanding, and the religious education of the children does not take the prominent place that it ought to have. Let each believing parent take Joshua's words— first in the depth of his own soul, then in fellowship with spouse and children. The more we speak it out in prayer and conversation—our house is and must be holy to the Lord, and our children must be trained first of all for God and His service—the more mightily will the power of the principle assert itself and help us so to guide the household that it, too, serves the Lord.

The words of Joshua teach us more. Let yours, like his, be a *practical* religion: "We will *serve* the LORD." There are many parents with whom the whole of Christian faith consists in salvation alone, not in service. They pray earnestly that all their children may be saved; if they see them spending their lives in the service of the world, they hope that they will still be brought to God before they die. It is no wonder that their education for this life has been a failure: the parents never understood the truth that training their children for God's service is the most certain way of bringing them to salvation. Didn't we hear God say of Abraham, "For I have chosen him, so that he will direct his children and his household after him to keep the way of the LORD by doing what is right and just, so that the LORD will bring about for Abraham what he has promised him" (Genesis 18:19)? And do we remember in connection with Israel's deliverance from Egypt the words God spoke: "Let my people go that they may *serve* me"? and Pharaoh's: "Go, *serve* the LORD; let your little ones also go with you"? And the Holy Spirit has spoken, "How much more shall the blood of Christ purge your conscience to *serve* the living God."

All redemption is for service. God does not will that He should be worshiped and not be served. The glory of heaven will be that "his servants serve him." Let our lives and our homes be consecrated to serving God: let obedience to His will, the carrying out of His commands, the doing of His work, and devotion to the interests of His kingdom give family life its focus.

Let your own be a *confessed* religion. It was in the presence of tens of thousands of the children of Israel, with the first symptoms of the falling away that came after his death already beginning to show themselves, that Joshua made this good confession: "Choose you this day whom you will serve . . . but as for me and my household, we will serve the LORD." His was not the religion of the nation or of the neighbors—all might reject God, leaving him alone, and yet still the Lord Jehovah would be his God. As concerning Abraham's leaving his father's house and Israel's leaving Egypt, his too was to be a religion of decision and confession—a coming out and being separate, a special people unto the Lord.

This is the religion we want in our family life, where not the example or authority of dedicated people, not inclination or pleasure, but God's own holy and blessed will is sought after as the law of the house. How often parents, whose early married life was marked by decision and earnestness, have afterward become conscious of declension and coldness because they gave in to the desire to gratify their children or their friends. Though at first sight it may appear hard to be different, if we trust God for His guidance and yield ourselves to His personal friendship and love to walk with Him, the blessing of separation will be unspeakable to us, and to our children too.

If there are parents reading this who are conscious that their own household's service to God has not been as marked and clear as it should be, let me give a word of advice. Talk about it among yourselves. Speak out what you have often felt but might have kept to yourself, that it is your united desire to live as entirely for God as grace can enable you to do. If your children are old enough, gather them together and ask if they will not join in the holy covenant: "We will serve the LORD." Let the covenant from time to time be renewed in a distinct act of consecration, that the conviction may be reconfirmed: We do not want to be just another family with whom God dwells and is pleased. Ours must be wholly consecrated to God. And do not be afraid that strength will not be given to keep the vow. It is with the Father in heaven, calling and helping and tenderly working both to will and to do in us, that we are working. We may count upon Him to inspire, to help, and even to carry out the purpose of our heart: "As for me and my household, we will serve the LORD."

PRAYER OF CONSECRATION

O Lord my God, I thank you for what I have seen this day in your servant Joshua, the leader of your people Israel into Canaan, in his faithfulness to you as father in his own home. I humbly ask you to give me the grace to say as distinctly and as publicly as Joshua did whom he and his house would serve.

Lord, may mine be a personal faith. Let your love to me and my love to you be its inspiration and its joy. May my children see that it is with my whole heart that I serve you and that it has become a delight to me.

And may mine be a family faith, exercising its influence on my home, gaining and training all to walk with me. Lord, remove every inconsistency and any weakness that might hinder anyone from being wholly yours. May mine be a truly consecrated home.

Make my faith practical, serving you day and night in all I do. Let the one desire of our hearts be knowing you and doing your will, working for your kingdom, and seeking your glory.

Make our home a blessing to others, encouraging them to take a stand for you. Lord God, may your Spirit work mightily in the homes of all your people, that everywhere this confession may be heard loud and clear: "As for me and my household, we will serve the LORD." Amen.

CHAPTER 17

CONSECRATED PARENTS

"So Manoah asked him, 'When your words are fulfilled, what is to be the rule for the boy's life and work?'"

—Judges 13:12

An angel of the Lord had appeared to Manoah's wife to predict the birth of a child. He would be a Nazarite unto God from his birth and a deliverer of God's people. The first impression Manoah had upon receiving the news from his wife was that to train such a God-given child for God's service, God-given grace would be needed. He entreated the Lord, "O Lord, I beg you, let the man of God you sent to us come again to teach us how to bring up the boy who is to be born" (Judges 13:8). And when in answer to his prayer the angel came again, his one petition was, "What is to be the rule for the boy's life and work?" (v. 12). Let us consider the prayer, the answer, and the attendant blessings.

1. *Notice the deep sense of responsibility for the holy work of training a child as a Nazarite unto God.* The angel had already given Manoah's wife the needful instruction, but Manoah is so deeply impressed with the holiness of their calling as parents of this child that he asks for the angel to come again and tell them what to do. What a contrast this is to the thoughtless self-confidence with which many Christian parents undertake the training of their children. Is there an effort made to realize the

magnitude and seriousness of the task? Is there humble prayer for the preparation of the Spirit to equip them for it? And finally, is there true surrender to a life devoted to God as the only real qualification for training a child for God?

What would we think of a man who offered to manage a bank or to navigate an ocean liner who had no training to fit him for either? And what can be said of the presumptive attitude that feels no fear of taking responsibility for an immortal spirit of such priceless value? May all Christian parents learn from Manoah to confess their ignorance and helplessness and, like him, to commit themselves to seek the needed grace.

We see, further, how Manoah's sense of need found its first expression in prayer. He believed in the living God, the One who could hear his prayer. He also believed that where God gives a charge or a calling, He also gives sufficient grace to do the job right; and more specifically, that where God gave a child to be trained for His service, He would also give the wisdom needed to train that child. Instead of allowing his sense of unworthiness and unpreparedness to depress him, or the weight of his obligation to push him to do it in his own strength, he simply prayed. Apparently, to him, prayer was the solution when faced with difficulties; it was the supply of need, the source of wisdom and strength.

Each child born to us is a gift of God as truly as was Manoah's and should be trained for God and His service. Like Manoah, we can be confident that the Father who entrusted the child to us will give the grace and enabling to train him. But let us pray in faith, and without ceasing, each step of the way. God hears prayer, and certainly no prayer more than that of a parent seeking wisdom to train his child.

There is another interesting detail about Manoah's prayer: after his wife told him of the injunctions given by the angel, he still asked for guidance. He wanted to hear them for himself, to have full certainty and perfect clarity. God's Word gives full and plain directions as to the training of children. Our own experience or that of others may have supplied us with much information of value to aid us in our task, but all this does not diminish the need for prayer. We need renewed wisdom directly from above for the individual needs of each child. Daily prayer is the secret of training our children for God.

2. *What was God's answer to Manoah's heart-cry?* The story of Manoah teaches us that God loves to answer the desperate pleas of a parent. The angel had nothing new to communicate beyond what he had already said to Manoah's wife; and yet God sent him back because He would not leave the one who sought to know His will in the dark. The angel, having come once, encouraged Manoah to hope that he might come a second time. Those who have already communicated with God and received divine teaching about their children will be those who desire still more and pray earnestly for it.

The answer to Manoah's prayer contained no new revelation; it simply pointed back to the instruction already given: "Your wife must do all that I have told her. . . . She must do everything I have commanded her" (vv. 13–14). The answer to our own prayer may contain no new truth; no new thought may be impressed upon our minds. But the reinforcement of what the Lord has already spoken, the principles laid down in Scripture brought afresh to our minds, will help us to realize as never before that our children belong to the Lord and must be kept holy for Him. Parents are God's ministers through whose godly life the children are to be blessed.

What were the commandments that had been given and were now renewed? The angel spoke only of the life of the mother before the birth of the child: the Nazarite child must have a Nazarite mother. The sacrifices she must make that are mentioned in verses thirteen through fourteen speak of the separation required unto purity and holiness. This was God's secret for parental success. Education consists not so much in what we do or say but in *what we are,* and this is true not only when our children are of an age to see and judge but long before, even before their birth. In that holy time of mystery, when mother and child are still one, the spirit of the mother is able to influence the child in the womb. Her relationship to God is important to the baby even then. For the child's physical well being, a mother will do things in moderation, denying herself certain foods or activities and resting more than is her usual habit for the sake of the new life within her.

3. *The blessing that attended Manoah's prayer was something more than the answer.* There was the blessed revelation of God himself and the wonderful knitting together of the hearts of the parents. Before he left them, the angel of the Lord so revealed himself that Manoah said, "We have seen God" (v. 22).

When he asked the angel's name, the angel told him it was "beyond [his] understanding" (v. 18). An interpretation of this phrase is "wonderful." And *wonderful* is still the name of the parent's God—wonderful in His love, wonderful in His ways, wonderful in His work, wonderful in what He does for us as parents, and wonderful in what He does through us for our children. Let us worship the Lord, the God of all parents, whose name is Wonderful! And let our prayer, like Manoah's, end in praise and worship, in faith and truth.

How rich the blessing this revelation brought to the praying couple. What a picture the chapter gives us of the way in which father and mother are lovingly to help each other in all that concerns their children. Manoah's wife receives the message from the angel; immediately she tells her husband. He prays at once for more light and fuller revelation. The angel comes again to her; she runs to tell Manoah, who follows her. He hears again what his wife had been told. When the sacrifice was offered and the angel ascended in the flame (v. 20), Manoah and his wife looked on together, and together they fell on their faces to the ground. And when Manoah was afraid, saying, "We are doomed to die! We have seen God!" (v. 22) she comforted him and helped strengthen his faith.

What blessed fellowship of love and faith, of prayer and worship between husband and wife, the responsibility of a child brings. The parents bless the child and the child blesses the parents. As they talk together about God's promises and His commands, as each tells the other what God has revealed in private prayer, and as they unite in seeking to know and carry out God's will, a stronger union is created. As they pray in each other's presence and worship the One whose name is Wonderful, they let go of their fears and encourage each other to trust and hope. Through these new experiences they will see that training a child is also training for the parents. Nothing opens the fountains of divine love and renewed love for each other more than the prayerful desire to know how to raise our children to love God.

PRAYER OF CONSECRATION

Blessed Lord, as those whom you have joined together to train our children for your holy service, we bow in united worship before you. Make us by your Holy Spirit to be so of one heart and mind that all you reveal to the one may at once be witnessed to the other. Grant that in our conversations and our prayers, in our weaknesses and fears, in our faith and our worship, we may learn to depend on one another and to trust each other to tend the children you have so graciously given to our care.

Lord God, we come to you now for wisdom to lead each child—each unique, each with different needs. For each one we ask, "What is to be the rule for the [child's] life and work?" Open our eyes to see the treasures of wisdom in your Holy Word, in promise and instruction for parents and children. Especially reveal yourself to us as the God of the covenant and of the promise, the God whose name is Wonderful. Teach us in holy fear and reverence, in childlike trust and joy, in purity of life and separation from the world, to walk before you, and so to train children that are yours, holy to the Lord, prepared to fight for the kingdom, to announce to the world your plan of redemption. Amen.

Chapter 18

A Consecrated Child

"I prayed for this child, and the LORD has granted me what I asked of him. So now I give him to the LORD. For his whole life he will be given over to the LORD."

—1 Samuel 1:27–28

The communion between the believing parent and the Lord in reference to his child has been set before us in the Word under different circumstances. In Samuel's story, we have a beautiful expression of the relationship between a mother and her child. Hannah has received a child from the Lord in answer to her prayer. The love and joy in her heart can find no better expression than in giving her child to the Lord again to be the Lord's as long as he lives. Whether we are thinking of God, of our child, or of ourselves, there is every reason to say, "For his whole life he will be given over to the LORD."

Doesn't the child already belong to God? Wasn't it to bear His own image, as His servant, for His own glory, that He created man—and that he allowed my child to be born? God looks upon him as His; he is only on loan, entrusted to me to teach and to train. Because I am naturally inclined to forget this, to love and treat the child as if he were mine alone, I count it a precious privilege, a distinct act of surrender, to give him to the Lord for all the days of his life.

God not only has a right to the child, but He needs him. The work He has to do on the earth is so great and He has so arranged for each to do his work that He cannot do without a single one of His people's children. We have heard of mothers who joyfully sacrificed an only son, or all her sons, for her king or for her country. Shouldn't we count it an honor to give to *our King* the child that is already His—whom He has loaned to us and given the privilege of loving and training while we fully enjoy him? Haven't we often asked what we can give back to Him for His great love for us? Shouldn't we delight to give to Him our most precious possession on earth? To Him who gave His Son for me, all I am and have belongs. I give my child to the Lord for as long as he lives.

It is not only for God's sake that I give my child to the Lord, it is for his sake too. The more I love him, the more eagerly I give him to God. Nowhere can he be more safe or happy than with Him. What I can do for my precious little one is limited. If I give him to God, I know that He will accept him and take him for His own. He will make him one with His beloved Son, cleansing him in the precious blood, and in rebirth by His Spirit, give him a new and holy nature. Almighty God will adopt my child as His! And he will use me as His minister, giving me all the wisdom I need to train my child on earth.

This commitment benefits me too. The child I give to God becomes doubly my own. I can love him with a more intense and holy love. I can hold him without the fear of losing him. Even if death were to take my child from me, I would know that he was serving in the King's own palace. God gave him to me; I gave him back to God. God gave him once again to me; and once again I gave him back to Him. Offering my child to God has become the link of a most blessed friendship and fellowship between God and me.

Let us consider how this consecration of the child is to be maintained and carried out in education. The grace promised for training a child is not given all at once but as it is needed, just as the grace for our own personal life is moment by moment. In the education of our children, difficulties will often arise, and sometimes it seems as if God's help is not forthcoming. This is the time for prayer and faith. The power of sin may manifest itself in the child, so that at times we are more fearful than hopeful. Our own ignorance or unfaithfulness or weakness may cause us to fear that although God is faithful, we may be the cause of our child's being lost. At such times, as at all times, God must be our refuge. Let us maintain our consecration of the child. We gave him to the Lord; we hold to this; and we refuse to take him back. This declaration will become in our souls a settled thing. What we gave, God took. The child is His, and we can leave him with Him with full assurance of hope. Such faith will give rest and bring certain blessing.

Let us make this known to our child too. Even if we don't often say it in words, he should know by our relationship with him that he has been given to God. Let him know that this is the reason we cannot give in to his will or allow sin to take control— we have a charge from God to train him for the kingdom. Let him see by our gentleness and firmness that this commitment is not a mere profession but a principle that motivates us. Eventually it will motivate him too. How can one who has been given to God disobey or grieve Him? By our life and prayer and education make the child know that he is the Lord's.

Allow this knowledge to be a constant reminder in the faithful discharge of our duties. The pressing occupations of life, the spirit of the world around us, and the meager direction we receive in regard to the education of our children make even godly parents grow weary or negligent. A consecrated education requires a high degree of devotion in our daily life. Let us stir ourselves to diligence, to faith, and to prayer.

God needs servants for His temple; let us ask Him what place He has for our child in His kingdom. If such a spirit motivated each parent who has given his child to God, there would be a much greater number of young people entering Christian service. If parents were as willing to consecrate their children as Hannah, who gave up Samuel to serve the temple, we would have no lack of men and women to serve in God's harvest fields. May God by His Holy Spirit teach us the full implication of our commitment: "I have given my child to be the Lord's as long as he lives."

PRAYER OF CONSECRATION

O Lord my God, hear, I pray, Hannah's prayer as I come to you with the child you have given me. I know that you allow a mother to give her child to you so that you can entrust him to her again. Having done so, he is yours and mine! My soul bows down at the thought of this inexplicable privilege, this joint ownership of my child. I look to you for the grace to keep this treasure for your glory and service.

Teach me, I pray, to love him with a holy love and to train him for the service of your temple. Teach me always to speak to him of your love so that his heart will early be won to you. May my whole life be an inspiration, guiding him to what is pure and lovely, to what is holy and well pleasing to you. In your great goodness, cause my child early to hear your voice and in childlike simplicity and reverence to answer, "Speak, Lord, for your servant hears."

O Lord, do not despise a mother's prayer. Accept my surrender. By your strength and blessing we will be consecrated parents of a consecrated child. Amen.

CHAPTER 19

PARENTAL WEAKNESS

"Why do you ... honor your sons more than me. . . ? Those who honor me I will honor, but those who despise me will be disdained."

—1 Samuel 2:29–30

"For I told him that I would judge his family forever because of the sin he knew about; his sons made themselves contemptible, and he failed to restrain them."

—1 Samuel 3:13

Some men are born to rule. It requires no real effort because it is their nature; they often do it unconsciously. To others it never comes naturally. They either shrink from it, or in attempting it they utterly fail. They appear to be lacking in the gifts that would equip them for the work; it is always a struggle and a concentrated effort. In ordinary life men choose or are chosen for the situations in which they fill roles as rulers or leaders. In family life, we see a very different set of circumstances: every parent has to rule whether he is fit for it or not. Nor does the fact of his uneasiness eliminate his responsibility; the distinct consequences of his failure to lead still fall upon him and his children. The picture of tottering old Eli, faithful to God's cause and ready to die for the ark of God, but unfaithful to his duty as parent—unable to restrain his sons—suggests to us the causes, the consequences, and the cure for parental ineptitude.

1. *We have spoken of the natural incapacity for ruling as one cause.* But this is never so absolute that determined effort could not to some extent remedy it, much less that the grace of God could not change it. We must therefore look for other causes. And of these the primary one is the lack of self-discipline. A Christian is not at liberty to follow the path of least resistance; that is, what he likes or what appears possible. He must ask himself: What is my duty? What has God commanded of me?

There is wonderful strength, even for the weakest character, in giving one's self up to the divine obligation to do God's will. The fear of grieving the Father, the desire to please Him, and the assurance of His strength to aid our weakness—such thoughts stir and quicken the energies of the soul. The will comes alive, and nothing is so invigorating as the honest effort to obey. Because some Christian parents do not realize that ruling their homes well is a simple matter of duty, a command that must be obeyed, many children are spoiled by parental permissiveness. Not to restrain a child is to dishonor God and the child.

Closely connected with this is the good-natured weakness—misnamed kindness—that cannot bear to reprove, deny, or punish a child. This is nothing but a form of sloth: it cannot take the trouble to rule and guide the child by God's Word, refusing the pain that discipline causes the parent. But it chooses the greater pain of seeing the child grow up out of control! No grace of the Christian life is obtained without sacrifice; this high privilege of influencing and forming other souls for God requires special self-sacrifice. Like every difficult work, it must have a purpose, attention, and perseverance behind it.

But the chief cause of parental failure is found deeper still: the lack of a life of true devotion to God. God is the great Ruler and Educator; the powers that be—including parents' powers—are ordained of God; he who does not live under the command of God in his own life does not have the secret of authority and command over others. The fear of God is the beginning of wisdom, including wisdom for the work of leading a family.

2. *Let's take a look at the consequences of parental weakness.* There is one element in the law of consequences under which we live that makes it especially serious. It is this: Ordinarily consequences are not experienced until it is too late to correct the cause. Our actions are seeds; no one who looks at a tiny seed can ever quite imagine what a great tree or what sweet or bitter fruit could come from it. Consequences seen in those around us somehow hardly affect us; self-interest flatters itself with the pleasing hope that, at least in our case, the results will not be so disastrous.

Let me plead with parents who have been guilty of consulting the will of their children more than the honor of God to look at Eli and his home under God's judgment. Let them ponder carefully what God says. Let them remember that throughout the universe there is no well-being but what is in harmony with the law of our being. On earth and in heaven, in nature and in grace, in the individual, the family, and the church, obedience to God's law for His creatures is the only way to happiness. To disobey that law is to court misery. And if parents, destined by God to bear in the home His likeness as a fatherly ruler, give way to permissiveness, they must expect the natural results.

It may not always become manifest to the same degree or with the same timing, but in the loss of their child's character, in the loss of peace and happiness—in many cases the loss of a soul forever—parents must reap what they sow. God appointed parental rule in the family as a type of His own authority, in which parents and children alike are to honor Him; to dishonor Him is to lose His favor and blessing.

3. *In speaking of the causes, we have already indicated some of the cures for parental weakness.* To continue, the first one is this: the determined purpose, by God's grace, to do God's will. My duty is never measured by what I feel is within my power to do

but by what God's grace enables me to do. And I can never know fully how much grace will allow me to do until I begin. Let the weak parent accept this as a God-imposed duty: He must rule his children. Let him remember that not to rule and restrain his children means both parent and child dishonor God. Let him yield himself to the God of grace with the purpose to do His will, however impossible it may appear; the surrender will be accepted and the grace not withheld. Step by step, amid many a failure, the honest effort to do God's will not go unrewarded.

Next, let the parent who has failed study some of the simplest laws in the art of leading. Ignorance and neglect of these are often the cause of failure. Ruling or leading, like any other art, must be learned.

Some of these rules are as follows:

- Do not give too many commands at once; begin, if need be, with only one. If you secure obedience to one, your own and the child's consciousness of your power to rule is established.
- Do not command what you cannot enforce or what the child has no power to obey.
- Prove your authority when it is easy for you to secure obedience and for the child to render it. In all learning we proceed from the easy to the less easy.
- Let the command be given in quiet, deliberate tones, with full self-control; hasty, ill-regulated injunctions lead to disobedience.
- Self-rule is the secret of all rule; as you honor the law in self-command, others learn to honor it too.
- Above all, let the Christian parent who would rule well remember that he is God's minister doing God's work. God loves the children and wants them trained for himself. He is your covenant God; depend upon Him to be your help and strength. It is God who, through you, will rule your home. Yield yourself to Him.

- Pray not only for help but believe that it will be given. And then act on the assurance that it is given and is beginning to work itself out in you. Say to your Father that you desire to do your duty at any cost and to honor Him with your children. And in the spirit of a quiet, restful assurance, you may count on God's strength working through your weakness.

PRAYER OF CONSECRATION

O my God, with fear and trembling I bow before you, the righteous God who does not give His honor to another nor allow sin, even in His servants, to go unpunished. Impress deeply upon my heart, O Lord, the solemn lessons you teach your church through the awful display of your judgment on the house of Eli.

Not to rule and restrain our children but to give them their own way is to honor them more than you. Before we think about it, weakness becomes wickedness, in ourselves and in our children. You have made every parent after your image, a king in his home, that he may rule his house well and command his children in the ways of the Lord. You have made your blessing dependent on our exercise of authority and our children's rendering of obedience.

O God, have mercy upon us! Let the thought of your command to rule our home, of your judgment on disobedience, of your promised grace to those who give themselves to obey, and of your blessing on a home ordered in the fear of God, stir us with our whole heart to fulfill our holy calling. And let us, above all, believe that as we and our children do your will, we are in the path of true blessing for this life and the life to come. Amen.

CHAPTER 20

THE FATHER AS INTERCESSOR

"When a period of feasting had run its course, Job would send and have them purified. Early in the morning he would sacrifice a burnt offering for each of them, thinking, 'Perhaps my children have sinned and cursed God in their hearts.' This was Job's regular custom."

—Job 1:5

What a beautiful picture of a man in whose heart the fear of God dwells! His greatest concern is that his children not sin against God or forsake Him in their hearts. He is so deeply conscious of the weakness of their nature that, even when he does not know of a positive transgression, the very thought of their having been in circumstances of temptation makes him afraid for their souls. He so fully realizes his position and privilege as father that he calls for them to be sanctified and takes upon himself the continual offering of the needed sacrifice. Job is another example among Bible saints of a servant of God in whom faith makes its home and by whose intercession and fear of God his children are redeemed. God could hardly have said of him, "There is no one on earth like him; he is blameless and upright, a man who fears God and shuns evil" (Job 1:8), if this element of true holiness had been lacking. The book might have been complete without it as far as the record of Job's patience and faith is concerned, but we would have missed the much-needed lesson that a man's entire consecration to God implies the consecration of his family life too. Let us study the lesson his example teaches.

1. *A deep fear of finding sin in himself or his children is one of the marks of a godly parent.* It was to conquer and make free from sin that God entered into the parental covenant with Abraham. It was because of sin, and to deliver from its root, that the blood of the lamb was sprinkled in the Passover. It was to lead out of sin and into the service of God that parents were appointed instructors of their children. In all God's dealings with us in redemption and in grace, in His revelation through Christ and His cross, He has had one objective: to save us from sin and to make us partakers of His holiness. If the parent is to be God's co-worker, if the authority God delegates to him is to be used correctly, and if the blessing promised him is to come to pass, God must find the parent in harmony with himself, hating sin with a perfect hatred and seeking, above all, to keep it out of his home.

But our views of sin are often superficial. How easily we are satisfied that all is well! Under the appearance of what is good and loving, sin may be lurking. Our children may be growing up quietly renouncing God in their hearts! Parents must ask God to give them an accurate sense of what sin is in their children—its curse, its dishonor to God, and its power.

We must ask Him to work in us a very deep and clear conviction that His great objective in taking us into covenant as His ministers to the children is that they may be delivered from sin. This is His one aim: that the power of Christ's victory over sin may be seen in the children, and our homes may be holy to the Lord.

2. *Careful watchfulness where there is certain to be temptation will be the natural result of such an aversion to sin.* Job knew that at a time of feasting there would be certain temptations for his

sons. When these days were past, he sent for them and sanctified them. These young men surely received a strong impression of the awfulness of sin by the action of their God-fearing father, such that a kind of watchfulness would be awakened in them and a fear of forgetting God. Every thoughtful parent knows that there are times and places when the temptations of sin will be more apt to surprise even the most well-behaved child. Such are the times, both before and after a child goes into a situation or circumstance where he may be tempted, that a praying father and mother should do what Job did, bring the children before God in repentance and faith and where possible to confront them with questions concerning their behavior.

A Christian man, recently converted, told of the indelible impression made on him by his mother when she sat him down, just before he was to happily embark on his first long journey away from home, and prayed with him that he might be kept from sin.

Let us ask God to make us very watchful and very wise in availing ourselves of opportunities to admonish our children and to pray audibly with them. There are times when the conscience of a child is especially sensitive and a word fitly spoken will sink deeply into the heart. There are also occasions when the conscience has been ignored and a word of prayer will help to awaken it and restore its authority. A parent in sympathy with God's purpose for destroying sin, and who holds himself at God's disposal, will be guided as to when and how to stir and strengthen in his child the consciousness of sin and its danger.

3. *A godly parent has power with God to intercede.* Job not only spoke to his children but he also sanctified them through burnt offerings, as was the custom. The parent who has accepted the sign of the sprinkling of the blood for his child and who has applied the blood on the doorposts of his home, has a right to plead with God on behalf of that blood covering. His faith ob-

tains pardon for the child—he can intercede for the grace that can save and sanctify.

We have, through the whole course of God's dealings with parents, from Noah forward, seen that God gives the parent the right and the power to appear and to act on behalf of his child and that such representative action is accepted. To grasp hold of the power of this is the very essence of parental faith; to act upon it is the secret of parental authority and blessing. The whole family dynamic is based upon this. All other influences a parent exerts depend on his being clear on this point: I am the steward of God's grace to my child; I represent my child with God and am heard on his behalf. This gives him confidence to say, I represent God to my child; I have authority and influence with my son or daughter because of my relationship to God. I have overcome the power of my child's sin by pleading with God for him, and together we shall conquer its manifestation.

Dear parents, let us earnestly plead that God by His Spirit will enlighten our hearts to understand our calling to intercede and prevail for our children. In our family's life, the first thing of importance must not be our earthly happiness, or even the supply of our daily needs, nor seeing to the children's education for a life of prosperity and usefulness, but rather the yielding of ourselves to God in order to be conveyors of His grace and blessing to our children. Let us live for God's purpose: deliverance from sin. Thus our family life will forever be brightened with God's presence and with the joy of our heavenly home to come, of which our earthly one is but the nursery and the image.

PRAYER OF CONSECRATION

Gracious God, I humbly ask you to stamp deeply in my heart the lessons your holy Word was given to teach. May Job, who has taught your saints so much about patience in the hour of trial and of your wondrous grace in delivering from it, be to all parents a role model of one who fears God.

Impress on us, we pray, the fear of God in its full extent and power, sorrowing over the sins of our children and interceding for them as for our own soul. Teach us, Lord, to abhor sin, the one thing you hate, and may we make it our aim to keep our children from its enticement and destruction.

May we realize our God-given position as intercessors and plead the blood for them as we do for ourselves, having full confidence that our prayers are heard.

Teach us to bring them with us in prayer, praying at the right time and in the right way, that from us they may learn both the fear of God and the confidence of faith. O God, if we are indeed your children, may these traits produce holiness in us and thus mark our home and family life as belonging wholly to you. Amen.

CHAPTER 21

THE TRUE GOOD

"Come, my children, listen to me;
I will teach you the fear of the LORD.
Whoever of you loves life and desires to see many good days,
keep your tongue from evil and your lips from speaking lies.
Turn from evil and do good; seek peace and pursue it."
—Psalm 34:11–14

There is a science called ethics that seeks to discover the laws that regulate human conduct, thus teaching the art of living right. In the pursuit of its objective, this science seeks to find out the motivating principle that urges men to act as they do—in other words, their purpose in life. In the discussions on this point, the word that comes up repeatedly is the *good*. Men propose to themselves some good or other as the reward of their efforts.

Students of ethics are divided into two schools, depending on the meaning they attach to the word *good*. With some, it expresses the good of *well-being*, the possession or enjoyment of what is desirable. They maintain that happiness—aversion to pain and desire for pleasure—is and ought to be the principal motive of conduct.

Another school takes higher ground. It maintains that although the desire for happiness is innate and legitimate, it may not be man's first or ultimate goal. Happiness will be the accompaniment and reward of something higher. The good of *well-doing* not of well-being is the only true good. The ideas of right and wrong are deeper and holier than those of pleasure and pain. To teach men to do good is the ideal.

In the words of our psalm, children are invited to come and learn the secret of a happy life. The call appeals to the desire for happiness: Who is he that would *see good?* The teacher promises to show the path to the enjoyment of true well-being. That path is marked, "Turn from evil, and do good." God has so ordered our nature that well-being will follow well-doing: to *do* good is the sure way to *see* good.

But our inspired teacher goes further. He not only tells of our *seeing* good and *doing* good, but also would teach us the secret of *being* good. Human science cannot teach this. The value of uprightness and purity in the inmost being, making conduct truly good, can be taught but it cannot show us what the true, the only pure and purifying, motive is. The psalmist tells us, "Come, my children, listen to me; I will teach you the fear of the LORD"—the beginning of all wisdom and goodness. It is our personal relationship to God that makes conduct truly good. To fear God—this is being good; then follows doing good; then seeing good.

Christian parents have in this call, "Come, my children, listen to me," words prepared for them by the Holy Spirit to use with their children. They are God's ministers to teach their children the fear of the Lord, the path to the true and highest good.

To begin with, *seeing good*: "Whoever of you loves life and desires to see many good days. . . ." Parents need not be afraid of promising their children that all will be well with them if they fear God. With a Creator of infinite goodness and wisdom it cannot be otherwise; doing right and pleasing Him will bring blessing and happiness. The desire for happiness may not be the first or the only motive for a man's conduct. Experience has proven that those who make it their first object fail, while those who give it second place, subordinate to duty, find it. God commands us to be happy. He promises us joy, but always in connection with our being in right relationship to himself and His will. So the previous verse (v. 10) says, "Those who seek the Lord lack no good thing."

The promises that God will do us good are many. To Jacob, he said, "I will surely do you good." And to Israel: "Do right and good that it may be well with you." His peace and presence, His guidance and help, will come to those who do His will. Such obedience and good works will bring a blessing even in this life.

Let our children learn early that if they would *see good*, it is found with God. Let them learn it from us, not as a doctrine, but as a personal testimony. Let us show them that service to God makes us happy and that the good that God bestows should be our one desire and our highest joy.

The next step is *doing good*. Let us endeavor to link insepa-rably well-doing and well-being in the hearts of our little ones. "Blessed is the man that fears the Lord." The Christianity of our day seeks safety in religion, but pleasure and happiness in the world. A very clear testimony is needed to show our children that to do God's will and serve Him is in itself pure blessing and enjoyment.

What is doing good, exactly? "Keep your tongue from evil and your lips from speaking lies. Turn from evil and do good; seek peace and pursue it." Sins of the tongue, sins of disobedi-ence, sins of temper—these are the three principal temptations for children. Parents have their work cut out for them to guard little ones from these.

"Keep your tongue from evil and your lips from speaking lies." The tongue reveals what is in the heart. Parents, study above all else to make your children true—first in word, then in heart, and finally in deed. A child's truthfulness and integrity may be the beginning of his walking in the truth of God. "I have

Caldwell
3 John 4

no greater joy than to know that my children walk in the truth." Let this be your aim, even with the little children.

"Turn from evil and do good." To a young child, evil is that which his parent forbids. The parent is to him a conscience, like God. Train your young ones to flee from evil, to depart, to come away from everything that is naughty or forbidden. Then keep him occupied with what is good, that which is allowed by you and pleasing to you. Stir and strengthen his young will, train him to *do* good—not to think and wish and feel good, but to do it. It is the will, and what it does, that makes the man.

7. 20/07

"Seek peace and pursue it." To quarrel is a sin that comes easily to children. Let us train ours to respect the rights of others, to bear and to forgive when our own are offended, seeking amends only from the parent. "Blessed are the peacemakers, for they will be called the children of God." *Matt 5:*

Of course, the highest goal is not to seek good or to do good but to *be* good. Only a good tree can bring forth good fruit. And what is it to be good? What is the disposition that makes a good adult or a good child? The fear of the Lord. There is none good but God; if we seek and find Him we find all that is good. It is in the fear of the Lord that good conduct has its source, that virtue has its worth. "In singleness of heart, fearing God: whatsoever you do, do it heartily, as unto the Lord." Our personal relationship to God carried out in all our conduct constitutes the fear of the Lord. It is not the fear of a slave, of course, but of a child, fear that is companion to hope and love: "The Lord takes pleasure in them that *fear* him, in those that hope in His mercy."

7. 20/07

Col 3:24

How can the fear of the Lord be taught? Christian parents know the answer: by walking in the fear of the Lord yourself each and every day. Seek to train your children to understand the connection between *seeing good*—always being blessed and happy—and *doing good*, where we always choose what is right. Finally, teach what *being good* entails: having a heart filled with the fear and love of God. Let them see you walk in the fear of the Lord, His holy presence resting on you and carried with you into daily life. Let them see in your conduct that your faith is more than a holy sentiment or emotion, that it is a power in the heart that activates the will in everything to do what is good. Let the light in your eyes and the smile on your face be the expression and confirmation of God's truth: "Blessed is the man that fears the Lord."

PRAYER OF CONSECRATION

Dear God, I ask for grace to wisely apply the lessons of your Word in dealing with my children. May my whole relationship with them be full of the joyful assurance that the fear of the Lord is the path to the enjoyment of all that is good, and that your service is true happiness. Let this be so real to them that all thought of pleasure in the world or sin may be far from their hearts.

Help me to teach them the fear of the Lord by instruction, example, and the spirit of my own life. May thoughtfulness, truthfulness, and lovingkindness mark the conversation of my home. May the life of all in my care be holy unto the Lord. Daily I would show them, through your grace, how departing from every evil, doing good, and following after peace and holiness is what true fear of the Lord produces.

Give me grace, above all, to teach them that the fear of the Lord is itself the true good and the principle behind it. May we walk as children in the full light of your countenance, fearful only of offending you or of not rendering the reverence due your holy majesty. Let ours be the true Christian life as followed by your disciples of old, who, walking in the fear of the Lord and in the comfort of the Holy Spirit, were multiplied daily.

My God, I beseech you, make me the parent you would have me to be and let your blessing abide on me and on my home. Amen.

CHAPTER 22

TRAINING

"Train a child in the way he should go, and when he is old he will not turn from it."

—Proverbs 22:6

This promise is the scriptural expression of the principle on which all education rests, that a child's training influences what his later life will be. Without faith in this principle there would be no reason to educate in the home. When this faith is elevated to a trust in God and His promises, it grows into the assurance that a parent's labor is not in vain in the Lord.

Education has been variously defined as fully developing a child's faculties, equipping him to fulfill his destiny, and developing in him all the perfection of which he is capable. Such definitions are valuable for every parent who would thoroughly understand his calling. Yet application of these methods is dependent upon the further statement of what the child's faculties and his destiny are and wherein his highest perfection consists. It is only when the real aim of education is clearly and firmly grasped that its work can be successful. Just as in our text, everything depends on a correct view of what "the way he should go" means. Only then can the training accomplish its work in the assurance of the divine fulfillment of the promise.

There have been so many failures in religious training that a

119

spirit of doubt has crept in as to whether a principle like this can be regarded as holding true universally. With such doubt we undermine God's covenant. Let us rather believe that any failure is owing to man's fault: "Let God be true, and every man a liar." Either the parent did not make "the way he should go" his true aim in the child's training, or the training in that way was not what God's Word intended it to be. Let's look at what the Word teaches on each of these points.

As to "the way he should go," there can be no doubt. The names Scripture gives to this way make clear what it is. God calls it "The way of the Lord" when He speaks of Abraham's training his children; we often read of "walking in his ways," "the way of his footsteps," and "the way of his commandments." It is called "the way of wisdom," "the way of righteousness," "the way of holiness," "the way of peace," "the way of life." This is "the new and living way," opened by Christ for all who will walk in His footsteps; it is Christ himself, the living Way, of whom Scripture says, "Walk in him."

There are many Christian parents who are anxious to see their children saved, but who do not choose this way for them. They do not decide on it early and concretely as the only way in which the children are to walk. They think it too much to expect of children to walk in it from their youth, and so they do not train them in it. They are not prepared to regard walking in this way as always the primary thing. It is not their first aim to train wholehearted, devoted Christians. There are worldly interests that must not be sacrificed. They are not always ready themselves to walk in "the narrow way"; they have chosen it, but not exclusively or finally. They have their own thoughts as to the way they and the child may go. No wonder that even with a great deal of apparent religious instruction, their education fails; a mistake here is often fatal. There can be no doubt or hesitancy; "the way of the Lord" must be heartily accepted as the only way in which their children should go.

"Train a child in the way he should go." *Train* is a word of deep importance for every teacher and parent to understand. Training is not telling, not teaching, not commanding, but something higher than all these (without which the teaching and commanding often does more harm than good). It is not only telling a child what to do but also showing him how to do it and then seeing that it is done, taking care that the advice or the command given is put into practice and adopted as a habit.

Look at the way a young horse is trained: It is made to yield its will to the master's until at last it is in perfect harmony with him and yields to his slightest wish. How carefully it is directed and *accustomed* to do the right thing until it becomes a habit, even second nature. Its own wild native tendencies are checked and restrained when necessary. It is encouraged and helped to the full exercise of its powers in subjection to this rule, and everything done to keep it bold and spirited. I have seen a coachman with thoughtful care watch his young horses, sitting ready at the slightest problem to help them by voice and hand lest they should lose their confidence or be overcome by some difficulty. And I have thought, *Oh, that parents bestowed this same care on training their children in the way they should go!*

Training may be defined: *accustoming the child to do easily and willingly what is commanded.* Doing right, doing it habitually, and doing it by choice—this is what we aim for.

Doing what is right. The parent who wishes to train not only tells or commands but also sees that the thing is done. To this end he seeks to engage the interest and affection of the child on the side of duty in general, as well as on a particular duty to be performed. Knowing how naturally thoughtless and wayward a child's nature tends to be, he urges or encourages until that which involves self-denial or difficulty is performed. He is careful not to give too many commands or to give them hastily; he begins with commands that are the easiest to submit to, so that the thought of obedience is not linked too much with what is displeasing or impossible to do. But the most important thing is that whether he appeals to the motive of authority or love, of duty or pleasure, he watches the child walk through the struggle until the consent of his will has become action and deed.

As we have said, *doing what is right habitually* is an element of training. Success in education depends more on forming habits than on inculcating rules. What the child has done once or twice he must learn to do over and over again until it becomes familiar and natural; it must feel strange to him *not* to do it. If the educator is content with only the early acts of obedience, then laziness, forgetfulness, reluctance to make an effort, flawed nature, and self-will may soon come in and break the power of the habit. The parent should silently watch, and if there is danger of retreat, he must help and confirm the habit until it is mastered. Going on from a first and a second command in which obedience has been secured, the principle is extended until the child comes to feel it quite natural that in everything he should do his parent's will. And so the habit of obedience is formed, and this becomes the root of other habits.

Doing what is right by choice. This is something higher, and is the true aim of education. You may have good, obedient children in whom there has not been much resistance to your training, and who render habitual and willing obedience. Yet when left to themselves later in life, these same children depart from the way in which they were trained. In these cases, the training was defective in that the parents were content with habits and not principles. The training of a young horse is not complete until he delights—full of joy and spirit—to do his work. It is the training of the will that is the aim of education. Beginning with *obedience*, the parent has to lead the child on to *freedom*. These apparent opposites have to be reconciled in practice, so that the child chooses and wills for himself what his parent wills, finding his happiness not only in obedience to the parent's command but in his own approval of the thing commanded—this is what the child must be trained to do. And here indeed is the highest art and the real challenge of training a child in the way he should go.

But here is where the promise of divine grace comes in. No mind completely understands the wondrous interaction of God's working and our working in the matter of our salvation—much less in the salvation of our children. But we need not understand it to be sure of it or to count on God's faithfulness. Where the believing parent seeks not only to form the habits of obedience, but also in prayer and faith to mold and guide and strengthen the will of the child in the ways of the Lord, he may count upon the workings of God's Holy Spirit to do what God alone can do. In covenant with God as His co-worker and minister, he does not shrink back from this highest and holiest of tasks, the training of a child's will made after the image of God's will. He counts on divine wisdom to guide him, divine strength to work with him and for him; he trusts in divine faithfulness to make the Word true and sure in all its fullness: "Train a child in the way he should go, and when he is old *he will not turn from it.*"

PRAYER OF CONSECRATION

Holy Lord, with fear and trembling I bow before you in light of the work to which you have called me—that of raising my child to love you. I know that I lack the necessary wisdom, so I come to you who promised to give it liberally and without judgment.

Lord, help me to understand fully the wonderful nature of the immortal spirit that you have placed in my care, with all its power of mind and emotion and will. Give me wisdom that I may know the way in which the child should go, even the way of your footsteps. May he learn from me that there is no other way well pleasing to you and thus no other way that can give true pleasure. Help me to guide and influence his will in such a way that he will yield himself first to my will and then to yours, to choose only and always your way.

And strengthen my faith, Lord, to hold onto the blessed assurance that a godly training in the fear of the Lord and under the rule of the Holy Spirit cannot fail. Your promise is sure; your power is infinite; you will bless the seed of your servant. Amen.

CHAPTER 23

CHOOSING THE GOOD

"But before the boy knows enough to reject the wrong and choose the right, the land of the two kings you dread will be laid waste."

—Isaiah 7:16

Of all the wondrous powers with which God has endowed man, his will—the power that determines what he does and, therefore, what he is—is the most wonderful. This is surely the deepest trait of the divine image. To a large extent, God gave man the power to decide what he will make of himself. The mind with all its marvelous capacities; the soul with all its wealth of feeling; the spirit, man's moral and religious nature—all these have been given that he might be able to exercise the royal prerogative he has from God: to choose—and so to fashion his own being and destiny for eternity.

To the parent is given the solemn task of teaching his child how to use this power rightly. This delicate instrument of direction and choice is placed into the hands of parents to guard, strengthen, and to train the child for the glory of God who gave it. Parents tend to shrink from the task, but if they will learn how wisdom can be gotten to train the child's will, they will likely count no sacrifice too great to secure it. To those who seek wisdom from God in faith and godly fear, success is possible, even promised.

The problem is a delicate one: it is to combine the greatest degree of personal liberty with the fullest exercise of obedience. God's Word teaches that obedience is the child's first virtue—that in doing so, he must exercise his will. He is to obey not because he understands or approves of the command but because it comes from his parent. By voluntarily submitting to a higher authority, he really becomes the master of his own will. While guiding the will into right habits, the command the child has over it is strengthened. When this has been attained, a safe foundation has been laid for exercise of the free will, when the child is older and on his own, in the selection of what appears to be the best choice, even when he may be strongly influenced to choose otherwise. This accomplishment is what the parent must regard as his highest and most blessed contribution to his child's development.

"Before the [child] knows enough to reject the wrong and choose the right . . ."—in this first stage of childhood, simple obedience is the law. As he grows older, it is still a parent's influence that trains the young will to exercise the power on which everything depends later in life. Because when he is on his own it will be entirely up to him to refuse wrong and choose what is right.

But how is this to be done? you may ask. The choices of the will depend upon deeply ingrained impulses and motives that prompt it to action. These impulses and motives depend upon what is presented to the young mind when it is most impressionable as well as the degree of attention that is given to them. Because of our fallen nature, the soul dwelling in the flesh and surrounded by the world, is far more alive to the visible and the temporal than to the unseen and the real. It is deceived by what appears pleasing or beautiful; the influence of the present outweighs that of the distant, even though it is of infinitely greater worth. It is the work of the parent, then, to present to the child what is pure and true and good. The beauty of virtue, the nobility and ultimate happiness of self-denial, the pleasure of responsibility, the fear and favor of God—not in these words, perhaps, but in those suited to a child's comprehension—the parent holds before him objects that awaken emotions by which the will is guided to gladly choose what is good.

Amid the thoughtlessness of childhood, which lives in the seen and the present, the parent acts as a conscience, calling the child to be true to his higher instincts and convictions and leading him to the pleasure with which duty rewards even the young. But the training of the child aims specifically at teaching him to refuse wrong and choose right when there is no parent near to help.

Of course, everyone possesses a guardian and helper of inestimable value in the path of right—one's own conscience. Wise training can do much to establish the authority of this inner rule, leading the child to look upon it not as a spy or a reproachful enemy, but as the truest friend and companion anyone can have. Let the authority of the parent and of conscience be linked together, that even in the parent's absence the weight of his influence may be felt. If the success of all true education consists in aiding the pupil to teach himself, the aim and success of moral training must consist of forming the habit of ruling oneself and always listening to the inward monitor. Cultivate in the child the power of self-control, of recollection, of quiet thoughtfulness, that he may always listen for the gentle inner whisper that tells him to refuse the wrong and choose what is right and good.

Conscience, however, can only tell to do right; what that right is it cannot always teach. The mind may be wrong in its views of good and evil, and faithfulness to conscience may even lead to choose evil and refuse good. The inner light shines upon the path of what we think of duty; it is only the light from above that shows what that duty is. "Your word is a lamp unto my feet and a light unto my path." One of the most precious influences of a godly education is not so much the knowledge of what the

Bible contains as the consent of the heart to take God's Word as the standard, desiring to let it decide in every choice. The authority of the parent, the conscience, and God's Word form a threefold cord that cannot be broken, binding the child to the throne and the will of God, there to know to refuse wrong and choose good.

1·07 prayer for Heidi ¹·²⁰

It is hardly necessary to repeat how such an education is not to take the place of divine grace, but rather to be its servant—both in preparing the way for God's Spirit by forming a strong and intelligent will to be afterward used in God's service, and in following up the work of grace by guiding it in the path where God's perfect will is accepted as the rule of conduct. Such training that equips the child always to make the right choice is of unspeakable worth. Let parents recognize the responsibility entrusted to them of awakening, guiding, and strengthening the young will on which such infinite issues depend, and know that if they can do this one thing well, they will have accomplished a priceless task. Inevitably, to choose good will be to choose Christ and holiness and eternal life.

God's highest gift to man in creation was the will, that he might freely choose the will of God. Your greatest challenge is to mold that will in your child and be God's minister in leading it toward salvation and His service. Pray earnestly for enlightenment for this holy trust committed to you. Study carefully the character of this endowment of the divine image. See in it the power to choose the gospel, Christ and His love, God and His service. Realize your incompetence to influence a will for which the powers of light and darkness are wrestling. Cast yourself on the covenant for the leading of the Holy Spirit, for the renewal of the Holy Spirit in your child, that it may be your joy and his to see his will given over to choose God.

PRAYER OF CONSECRATION

Lord God, how holy is the work you have committed to parents. Open my eyes, I pray, to see its awesome responsibility.

I see traces of the divine image in my child's will. Make the tremendous issues dependent upon the right use of his will for time and eternity be ever before me. I want to be conscious of the danger posed by sin within and temptations without. May I realize the wonderful power entrusted to me in your giving my child's will into my keeping. I am weak, but I know your almighty power is working in me to keep me humble yet hopeful, conscious of my weakness yet confident in you. O God, teach me to form and train the will of my child to refuse wrong and choose what is right.

Lord, make me very gentle and patient, and very watchful, because of the sleepless vigilance of the Enemy and the vulnerability of my child. May I be ever faithful to fulfill my commission well, full of trust because you are my help.

For Jesus' sake I ask these things. Amen.

CHAPTER 24

GOD'S SPIRIT IN OUR CHILDREN

"For I will pour water on the thirsty land, and streams on the dry ground; I will pour out my Spirit on your offspring, and my blessing on your descendants. They will spring up like grass in a meadow, like poplar trees by flowing streams. One will say, 'I belong to the LORD'; another will call himself by the name of Jacob; still another will write on his hand, 'The Lord's,' and will take the name Israel."

—Isaiah 44:3–5

In the prophecy of the outpouring of the Holy Spirit quoted by Peter on the day of Pentecost, mention is made of the sons and daughters; here too, in Isaiah, the blessing of the Spirit's outpouring is made to the seed and offspring of God's people. The root principle of the covenant, promising grace to the fathers for the children and to the children for the fathers, is to be the mark of the dispensation of the Spirit. Not content with a religion inherited from the fathers, the children would openly profess their personal faith: "I belong to the Lord." Through the power of the Holy Spirit the religion of parental training would become the faith of a personal profession. Let us seek to grasp the two thoughts: the personal acknowledgment of the Lord as the fruit of the Spirit's work, and the sure promise of the Spirit to do that work.

Among all Christian parents there is the desire that as their children grow up, they may come to make personal confession of the faith in which they have been raised. If we enter fully into the mind of God, it will become one of the great aims of our parental training to rear our children for such a profession. And yet there are many Christian parents who hesitate to admit this. To some the dangers attending a distinctly religious education, of cultivating a formal and traditional faith, appear so great that they leave their children almost to themselves—or to others. They would never think of asking them whether they can say that they belong to the Lord or even encourage them to do so. Quite simply, some do not believe in the conversion of children. They feel that children are so impressionable and so much the creatures of their surroundings that such a profession cannot be counted on and even ought to be avoided. Others are so much in doubt as to what they believe about the assurance of faith that, having themselves no liberty to say, "I belong to the Lord," it is no wonder they never think to help their children to reach that confidence. They think it is only the advanced believers who would dare to make such a bold confession; in them it would be presumption and pride. With still others, though they admit in theory to the duty of making such a statement and even to the possibility of a child making it, their hearts are so cold and worldly that the loving acknowledgment of Jesus as Lord never passes their lips. Family worship and religious profession testify to anything but the living, loving attachment to a personal Savior.

And yet we see promised so clearly in Scripture that the Spirit's working in us a living, spiritual faith will manifest itself in this way—by confession. Experience has proven to many who formerly were in doubt that a plain profession of Jesus as Savior is as sure a fruit of the Spirit's presence among children as it is among older people—and that it can be just as trustworthy. A little reflection will convince us that nothing is more natural than this fruit of God's blessing on the labors of believing parents. Don't we tell children from their youth that God is love and that He gave Jesus to be their Savior? Don't we tell them that they belong to God, not only by right of creation and redemption but by virtue of our having given them to Him before they were born? Why should it seem strange if the child believes what we say and speaks it out: "I belong to the Lord"? We tell them that Jesus receives sinners who confess their sins and give themselves to Him to be cleansed. What we ought to hope for as the fruit of our instruction is that when they feel sorry for their sins, they will go to Jesus and confess them, believing that He will not cast them out but accept and pardon them.

We must be very careful about casting suspicion on the child-like testimony. If their young hearts are touched and they express their love or commitment, who are we to doubt their profession or reproach them because they are young? Let us rather be confident of the promised fruit of the Spirit's working among our children.

On the other hand, we must not take every early confession as solid proof that a child is born again and there is no more need to explain or inquire further. Impressions may be temporary and professions superficial, especially with very young children. There will still be a need for teaching and gentle reminders to be obedient to the Word and love the Lord with all our heart. It is the work of the Holy Spirit that makes real any profession of faith.

The Spirit dwells in the church of Christ, in the hearts and the homes of His believing disciples. There may at times come special outpourings of the Spirit in revival movements of wider or smaller extent, when the young come forward in numbers to confess the Lord. But we don't have to wait for this. In promising the Spirit to the offspring of His people, God expects that parental instruction, a consecrated homelife, and faithful gathering with other believers will be the means the Spirit uses to lead the children to Christ. The Spirit always works through the

Word; to a child, the parent is the God-ordained minister of the Word. The blessing of the new dispensation is that the parent may count on the Holy Spirit for his children, from their youth up, and know that all his teaching and training, though it may be in weakness and in trepidation, will be in demonstration of the Spirit and of power.

But it all depends upon the parent as a minister of the Spirit. He must live and walk in the Spirit, he must be led and sanctified by the Spirit, he must speak and pray in the Spirit, and he must in faith claim and accept the promise of the Spirit for his child. As we have said, it is possible that a child's profession to belong to the Lord may be invalid. But this depends greatly on the parents and those who surround the child. He takes the meaning of his words from them. If to them it is the language of a joyous faith and consecration, the child unconsciously catches the meaning from the spirit in which he sees them live. If they watch over his innocence and eagerness and speak words of help and encouragement, even the little child can prove the reality of the change to which this profession attests.

Parents, let God's thoughts and desires for your children take hold of your hearts and rule there. Especially these two thoughts: (1) God's Spirit and my children belong to each other; I may in faith claim the Spirit's dwelling and working in them. (2) My child may know and say that he is the Lord's; the fruit of the Spirit is the faith of the heart and the confession of the lips, "Jesus is mine." Let this promise be your strength as you deal with God, your strength as you deal with your child: They that wait on the Lord shall not be ashamed.

PRAYER OF CONSECRATION

O Lord, we draw nigh to you to claim the fulfillment of this promise on behalf of our beloved children. Lord, may they from their very youth have your Spirit poured out upon them that even in the simplicity of childhood they may say, "I belong to the Lord."

Be pleased, Lord, to fill us, your servants, with your Holy Spirit. May our homelife and our parental influence be a channel through which the Spirit reaches each child. God, help us so to live that the life that breathes around our children may be life in the Spirit.

We pray especially for singleness of purpose in training our children for you alone—that the indwelling of the blessed Spirit may not be thought of as something rarely to be expected but as the one gift the Father loves to bestow and the first thing our children need in order to grow up into devoted Christians! Lord, let our training of them, as your exclusive sacred property, be our consuming desire. We know we can count on the fact that as we consecrate each one to you, by your Spirit, you will consecrate that one as your own. May we experience how wonderfully the parents' work and the Spirit's work blend in securing the seed of your people for your glory. Amen.

CHAPTER 25

FROM GENERATION TO GENERATION

"For the moth will eat them up like a garment; the worm will devour them like wool. But my righteousness will last forever, my salvation through all generations."

—Isaiah 51:8

When we speak of a generation in the history of man, we think of the shortness of human life and the continual change among men. "One generation passes away, and another generation comes: but the earth abides forever." What a contrast between man and the heavens above or the mountains around him—they are always the same. Even more so, what a contrast there is between man whose life is but a span and the unchangeable, everlasting God.

But we find in God's Word that these opposites all link together rather than contrast; man is lifted out of the transitory life to find his refuge in the unchangeableness of God. "As for man, his days are as grass . . . but the mercy of the Lord is from everlasting to everlasting upon them that fear him, and his righteousness unto children's children."

The psalmist said,

> In the beginning you laid the foundations of the earth, and the heavens are the work of your hands. They will perish, but you remain; they will all wear out like a garment. Like clothing you will change them and they will be discarded. But you re-

main the same, and your years will never end. The children of your servants will live in your presence; their descendants will be established before you. (Psalm 102:25–28)

Death may separate one generation from another, but God's mercy connects them as it passes on from one to another; His righteousness, which is everlasting, reveals itself as salvation from generation to generation.

At every point where God meets and acts with man, there are two sides to be regarded—the divine and the human. So it is in the transmission of God's salvation from generation to generation. God's faithfulness inspires that of man and therefore demands and rewards it. In some passages it might almost appear as if everything depended upon man and his keeping the covenant; and so it does. But not as if the keeping of the covenant were the means by which the blessing is secured. No, rather it is in the mercy and truth of God, and as these are known and trusted, human faithfulness has its strength and security. To know God's purpose, to believe God's promise, to adore God's unchanging faithfulness communicates to the soul the very spirit of that faithfulness and binds us firmly to Him, so that He who is all in all can work out His purposes in us.

Let us look first at the divine side of this salvation from generation to generation. In Isaiah we have the words that express this truth with great frequency and distinctness:

> In the beginning you laid the foundations of the earth, and the heavens are the work of your hands. They will perish, but you remain; they will all wear out like a garment. Like clothing you will change them and they will be discarded. But you remain the same, and your years will never end. The children of your servants will live in your presence; their descendants will be established before you. (Isaiah 59:21)

This speaks of New Testament times. When God made His covenant with David, He anticipated generations in which there would be disobedience and therefore punishment (2 Samuel 2:14; Psalm 89:30–33). But here the promise of the Spirit and the Word in the mouth of God's Anointed One and His people is not to pass from the mouth of the children's children. There are families in which for generations, even for centuries, the Word and the Spirit have not departed from the mouth of the seed's seed.

Then we have the other beautiful promise:

> For I, the LORD, love justice; I hate robbery and iniquity. In my faithfulness I will reward them and make an everlasting covenant with them. Their descendants will be known among the nations and their offspring among the peoples. All who see them will acknowledge that they are a people the LORD has blessed. (Isaiah 61:8–9)

Or, as it is otherwise expressed in Isaiah 65:23, "They will not toil in vain or bear children doomed to misfortune; for they will be a people blessed by the LORD, they and their descendants with them." The covenant with Abraham and David was also an everlasting covenant, but its fulfillment was reached over the heads of generations that proved faithless. Here, in the power of the promised Spirit, believing parents may claim and expect, from child to child, to see the blessing of the Lord. This is to be the fruit of the outpouring of the Holy Spirit; the promise, "You and your son and your son's son," is to have its literal fulfillment. This is not for our comfort and joy and the blessing on our children only, but that God may be known and glorified. "Their seed shall be known among the Gentiles." To be God's witnesses on earth—if need be, among the Gentiles to the ends of the earth— the Word and the Spirit are not to depart from the mouth of our offspring from now on and forevermore.

Let's look now from the human side at the fulfillment of this promise: "My salvation from generation to generation." Most strikingly God's purpose is set forth in the words of Psalm 78:4–7:

> We will not hide them from their children; we will tell

the next generation the praiseworthy deeds of the LORD, his power, and the wonders he has done. He decreed statutes for Jacob and established the law in Israel, which he commanded our forefathers to teach their children, so the next generation would know them, even the children yet to be born, and they in turn would tell their children. Then they would put their trust in God and would not forget his deeds but would keep his commands.

We read in Psalm 145:4, "One generation will commend your works to another; they will tell of your mighty acts." The triumphant joy of this psalm of praise is the spirit in which the parents tell their child of God's glory and goodness.

Here we have the human side. Parents who know God show His praise and His strength and His wonderful works to their children. Parental instruction is in the ministry of the Spirit more than in the old covenant, testifying for God in the spirit of praise and telling what He has done for us—His strength and His wonderful works. And so the children are taught not to forget the works of God, but to set their hope on Him and keep His commandments—to trust and to obey Him. And so His righteousness, which is from everlasting to everlasting, becomes salvation from generation to generation.

It is God's will that His salvation should be known from generation to generation in your family too, that your children should hear from you and pass on to their children the praises of the Lord. Let us enter into God's plans, and with our whole heart work earnestly to secure the blessing and to please our Father. We know what is needed—wholehearted devotion to God. Nothing less will do. God's salvation must not be a secondary thing, something to be enjoyed along with other things. It must be the primary thing. We must set our whole heart upon it, even as God does. It must be the one thing we live for, to glorify God. It is such a life that will prove to the children the joy of God's salvation, that it is a blessing and a delight. This will influence them to come along with us. It is this wholehearted devotion that will give strength to our faith and confidence to our hope. Under its inspiration our prayers will be persevering and believing. It will give to our instruction the tone of assurance that is needed and will make our whole life a role model for our children. It is one generation living for God that will secure the next for Him. So I can ask in faith, expecting that my wholehearted consecration to God will, in His infinite mercy, guide my children toward the same goal; His salvation is from generation to generation.

PRAYER OF CONSECRATION

Gracious Father, I bow before you once again with the prayer that you would open my eyes and my heart that I may fully comprehend your holy purpose for earthly parentage, transmitting through it your blessing. Lord, let your word, "My salvation is from generation to generation," so fill my heart that my calling and duty, with your promise and purpose, may be equally clear and that the salvation of my children will be as sure as my own.

And grant, Lord, that in your light I may realize and manifest fully what salvation is—salvation from sin and its power unto the holiness and the service of God. Let it be in me a salvation that fills my heart with gladness and my lips with praise; my whole life with purity and love. Let the salvation in which I walk and in which I train my children be not what man alone calls salvation, but be truly the salvation of God.

My God, I do beseech you, by your mercy, may this salvation be the one "heirloom" my children cherish, the one precious gift that is transmitted in our home from child to child, salvation that embraces the love, the joy, and the service of God. You, Lord, are the eternal and unchanging One; let it be so from generation to generation. Amen.

CHAPTER 26

THE CROWNING BLESSING

"I will pour out my Spirit on all people. Your sons and daughters will prophesy, your old men will dream dreams, your young men will see visions."

—Joel 2:28

This is the promise of which the day of Pentecost was the fulfillment and the interpretation. The coming of the Comforter, the baptism with the Holy Spirit and with fire, the endowment with power from on high to be His witnesses to the ends of the earth—all these precious promises of Christ were comprehended and fulfilled in Joel's prophecy. It contains the title deed to the birthright of Christ's church: the Holy Spirit from the throne of the exalted Savior, her power for testimony and for suffering, for triumph and for blessing, and the heavenly sign with which she has been marked and sealed.

See the place given to the children in this foundation promise: "Your sons and daughters shall prophesy, your old men will dream dreams, your young men will see visions." The seed of God's people has such a place in His heart that even in the promise of Pentecost the first thing introduced is not the disciples anointed to preach but the sons and the daughters prepared to prophesy. Let us attempt to take in what it teaches us of God's purpose, of a parent's hope, and of a child's education.

1. *God's purpose.* With the gift of the Holy Spirit to His church, God had an object: the power from on high for her work of testifying to the ends of the earth. The very last words of the Master (Acts 1:8) speak of this. All the other blessings of the Spirit—assurance, joy, holiness, love—have as their aim fruit-bearing and the power to bless. It is because many Christians do not understand this that there is often a weary and fruitless seeking for the blessings of the Spirit, when they would come naturally if there were but a wholehearted surrender to the Spirit. He is given to empower the Christian for God's service and work. No wise man wastes power; rather, he economizes it and uses only what is sufficient for the work. The measure and the power of the Spirit of God is given according to the work our will undertakes and our faith expects.

This is also true in our children. In Joel's prophecy, God reveals His purposes for our sons and daughters. Under the mighty breath of His Spirit they are to prophesy. Paul tells us what it is: "If an unbeliever or someone who does not understand comes in while everybody is prophesying, he will be convinced by all that he is a sinner and will be judged by all, and the secrets of his heart will be laid bare. So he will fall down and worship God, exclaiming, 'God is really among you!'" (1 Corinthians 14:24–25). This prophesying is in the power of the Spirit, convicting even the unbelieving and unlearned. And for this God wants our sons and daughters. Therefore, in this dispensation of the Holy Spirit, we need to educate our sons and daughters.

The world is in dire need of them. The church is suffering for want of workers. Supply always creates demand. Because there is such a small supply, the church thinks it has done something great when there is some annual increase in the number of its layleaders. But if there were truly a heart to enter into God's purposes, and the church and parents understood what a privilege it is to train our sons and daughters to be prophets of the Most High, witnesses and messengers for Jesus our Lord, what a change it would bring in our modes of operation! As the children of this nation do their utmost to obtain some high commission in the armed forces, some good appointment in civil service or in business, why shouldn't the children of God gather around the throne of their Father, seeking His favor in their children, making them His prophets wherever He has need of them? God's purpose is that the Holy Spirit should take possession of our sons and daughters for His service; that they should be filled with the Holy Spirit, consecrated for service. They belong to Him and He to them.

2. *The parent's hope.* Imagine what it would be like if believing parents entered fully and heartily into this purpose of God, acting upon it as a settled fact that they are training their children for His service. Would there be any doubt in their minds as to whether they might count on the conversion of their children? "Aim high" is a daily maxim; with it you will accomplish more than he who is content to let the day run its course. This is the blessing of full consecration: while it aims at the highest that God has promised, the secondary gifts, which others struggle all their lives to attain, fall to them effortlessly. Nothing will give such confidence for the salvation of our children, of the Spirit's working for conversion and renewal, as the knowledge of our having surrendered them unreservedly to the service of God and His Spirit.

This commitment will also increase our confidence in regard to fitness for parental duty. We have no concept of the extent to which self-interest weakens faith and self-sacrifice emboldens it. If I know I am seeking the salvation of my children for my sake and theirs alone, the soul cannot rise to the confident assurance that grace for training my child will be given. But let me put aside all selfish thought and place them at God's disposal, and it will become impossible to doubt that my Father will give me grace for the work I do for Him.

Though there is a diversity of gifts, and I may not see each child used in the direct service of the Master, I may be sure that my heart's purpose is to accept His will, and my effort to train my children to be the vessels of God's Holy Spirit has had its elevating influence on my own soul, on my home, and on each of my children, whatever their calling in life may be. The more distinctly I acknowledge to the family that in this dispensation the Spirit claims all, the more I can depend upon His presence with me and mine. Such a purpose in God's heart and such a hope in the parent's heart will influence the children's training.

3. *The children's training.* Cultivate every mental power, keeping in view the preparation of a sharp instrument for the Master's use. Encourage natural virtues—diligence and decision-making, order and method, promptness and dependability—with the ultimate aim of having the child more fit for the work to be done. Let obedience to conscience and to the law, self-control and temperance, integrity and justice, humility and love, be the goals in their education, that the Holy Spirit may nurture an efficient servant of the Lord.

The prize that parents seek for their children is often counted worthy of any sacrifice; there have been those who have willingly suffered lack of many good things to give their children a liberal education or to secure for them a position in the world. Let us so set our hearts upon the promotion we seek for our children that all thought of sacrifice is swallowed up in study and labor, prayer and faith, to have them counted worthy of a place among the separated ones whom the Spirit of the Lord anoints for His work.

Now we will conclude our meditations on the Old Testament testimony of the place children occupy in the purpose and promise of God. We have seen what God can be to our children—a God of covenant blessing by the blood and the Spirit of Jesus. And we have seen what He wants our children to be to Him—a covenant seed, to receive and transmit and multiply the blessing throughout the earth. And we know what their children can in turn become: ministers of the covenant, applying and pleading the blood with Him and receiving the Spirit from Him; by example and training and life communicating the blessing as channels for the Spirit's training of future generations for His service.

God help us to learn these three lessons pertaining to God's purpose, the parent's hope, and the children's training. May He help us to believe and receive all He is willing to be to our children through our lives, to seek for them nothing less than God seeks, and so to live that from our homes may go out sons and daughters to prophesy in His name.

PRAYER OF CONSECRATION

Lord God, we thank you again for the institution of the family, your divine appointment for transmitting salvation to all generations. And we thank you, too, for the revelation of yourself as the covenant God to the children of your servants, pledging yourself to fulfill all your promises of blessing. And we thank you most of all for the promise of the Spirit to dwell in our sons and daughters.

O Lord, fulfill your promise to our children. Give us grace to train them for you, believing in the Spirit's working, the Spirit's coming with power. Give us grace to prepare them for the Master's use, every natural and spiritual gift cultivated and consecrated for your service. May our sons and daughters prophesy in the power of your Holy Spirit.

And Lord, bless all believing parents. Let your claim on their children, the promise of the Spirit, the inconceivably high privilege of offering their children for service be the answer to the need for laborers. Fill their hearts with your love and peace that all their training may be in harmony with your grand purposes for our sons and daughters. Amen.

CHAPTER 27

THE HEAVENLY AND THE EARTHLY FATHER

"If you, then, though you are evil, know how to give good gifts to your children, how much more will your Father in heaven give good gifts to those who ask him!"

—Matthew 7:11

We began our meditations from the Old Testament with the home on earth a picture of the home in heaven. The glory of the New Testament is its fuller revelation of the Father in heaven. We can have no better beginning for our New Testament studies of what God intends family life to be than to see what light the fatherhood of God casts on our own fatherhood, on what we are to be to our children.

1. *First of all, we see how Jesus desires that we rise above the experiences of fatherhood on earth to know more deeply the Father in heaven.* Let us be clear on the fact that our fatherhood is not the original and the reality, but God is the first Father from eternity. By His very nature He is the God of love, a father to all by Creation and redemption. He is our example, our mentor in fathering. We are privileged to taste the blessedness of fathering a son or daughter in our likeness, having a child to be the object of our love, the reflection of our image, a companion and helper in all we do.

We must study the father heart on earth and from it gain a

truer and fuller grasp of what God is to us. Homelife is as much a school for training parents as for children. As we think of our love for our children—the joy they give us, the tender sympathy their troubles stir in us, the patient kindness their lethargy or waywardness requires, the ready response with which we meet their needs—Jesus wants us to look to Him and calculate *how much more* these parenting traits exist in God, the only perfect Father. He wants us to banish every shadow of unbelief from our heart and live our life in the sunshine and grace of His unconditional love.

As we see what influence a parent can exert on his child, breathing his disposition and even his will into him, securing his unbounded trust, He would have us be confident that the Father is able to breathe His own mind, His own disposition, His own Spirit, into us. And as we claim and strive to secure the love and obedience of our children, as we long that they should find their happiness in our will, our friendship, our company, He asks us to remember that the Father loves to meet us in secret, that the voice and the trust of His child are His joy and will meet a rich reward. What a parallel for every father and mother to see: each pulse of love and joy that swells their hearts marks the revelation of divine love and joy bending over them, longing to meet the response of their childlike love and joy.

2. *The fatherhood in heaven teaches us what fatherhood ought to be.* In giving us the place and the name and the power of fatherhood, God has in a very real and solemn sense made us His image-bearers. He asks and expects us, in doing our work, to copy Him, to act as closely like Him as possible. The parents who desire to bring a full blessing to their children must make God's fatherhood their role model.

They must enter into God's purpose and make it their own, giving themselves to pursue it with their whole heart. The heavenly Father seeks to educate children in *His likeness*. He has nothing higher to bestow on them. God has appointed parents on earth to be His ministers and fellow workers, to carry out His plan. How can they, unless they understand it and make its realization the first objective of family life?

From the Father in heaven they must learn, too, the way in which that purpose is to be attained. In His dealings with His people, parents will see how He came first in love and kindness, as with Abraham, securing trust and confidence; then with the law and its authority to lead on to self-knowledge and self-renunciation; then with the gospel of full liberty in the Spirit that we might no longer be children but grown men. From Him parents will learn to combine love with authority, and through these to aim at the free and full surrender to all of God's will. In the tenderness and patience and self-sacrifice of divine love, in the firmness and righteousness of divine rule, the parent will find the secret of successful training.

Above all, we must learn from the Father how personal such training is. How that the Father came down to us in Christ; how through His own example He shows us that He wants us to be as He is; how in giving us His Spirit He would have us to understand that fatherhood desires to draw the child into perfect likeness and oneness with itself. As the earthly father contemplates the heavenly Father's example, it will dawn on him that the highest duty of fatherhood is to be what we want the child to be. A father must breathe his own spirit into the child just as a child of the heavenly Father receives His Spirit day by day.

Isn't it an awesome thing to be a parent?

3. *The earthly father must not only make the Father in heaven his model and guide, but he must so reflect Him that his child will naturally desire to emulate the One whom he so aptly represents.* A child loves his parents by natural instinct; as the child sees in the father all that is holy and worthy of honor, the response is an affectionate and enthusiastic admiration. In a Christian father a child ought to have a better picture than the best of sermons can

give of the love and care of the heavenly Father and all the blessing and joy He wants to bestow.

But to attain to this the parent must consciously and distinctly aim at making himself and the name he bears the ladder by which the child can climb to the Father above. It is when the enthusiastic, cheerful countenance of the parents—a mingling of reverence for God with childlike love—is ever before the children from their earliest days that the name of *Father* will become linked with all that is lovely and holy in the memory. It is not simply a matter of reflection, but as the very life-breath of God is taken in unconsciously, the fatherhood on earth will have become the gate of heaven.

Is it really possible to live so that this becomes a reality? The one thing the Father loves to give, which is the sum and center of all His good gifts, is His Holy Spirit. We have but to believe, and as we believe, to receive, and as we receive, to yield to and live in the Spirit; He will make our fatherhood the image of God's, and from us will flow streams of living water to bless our children.

What a world it would be if every Christian father sought to realize and fulfill his calling and in his home as God's ambassador to bear the holy name of father—if in partnership with the Father in heaven, he yielded himself to be taught and sanctified and used to train his children to love God. Let us all who are fathers join together in partnership with our wives to pray fervently that the Father would make us all the worthy bearers of His name.

PRAYER OF CONSECRATION

Our Father who art in heaven, we unite in earnest prayer for all your children who bear the holy name of father. Give us more insight into your fatherhood and into the unspeakable riches for those who are included in your family. From the wonderful traits of your own likeness seen in our affection for our children, let us learn to believe and enjoy the divine fullness of love that your heart and your name offer. Let our own role as fathers teach us the blessedness of being the children of your Father-love.

Help us to see, Father, how you desire that our fatherhood should be nothing less than a reflection of yours. May our goals in this calling be one—in purpose, in method, in principle, and in spirit. O God, we want to be fathers to our children just as you are to us, so that you can fully use us as channels of your Father-grace to them. May they see in us a true picture of you.

We look to your Son for help and answer to our prayer. We count upon the tenderness and faithfulness of your love and upon your mighty power and Spirit to bless the parents of your church who cry out to you. Amen.

CHAPTER 28

CHILDREN OF THE KINGDOM

"But the subjects of the kingdom will be thrown outside, into the darkness."

—Matthew 8:12

The wonderful privilege and the awful danger that come with the place our children have in the church of Christ lie in close proximity. They are children of the kingdom—what could be more glorious! But they could be cast out into outer darkness— what could be more awful! The only way to avoid the latter is to fully grasp the former, to be sure that being a "child of the kingdom" is not only a title but also an experience that changes and renews the whole life.

When we say we are children of the kingdom, to what kingdom are we referring? The answer is simple: the kingdom of God. And where is this kingdom? Its origin is in heaven—the divine rule or dominion in the heavenlies, its center being the throne of God, on which He dwells. He is the Holy One from whom all life and law and love flow. Around that throne are powers and principalities and dominions, with their myriad holy angels who do His will and are the messengers of His power. The mark of this kingdom is that in God everything is love and blessing; in His subjects, everything is obedience and joy.

So how can this heavenly kingdom be here on earth? When

God created the heavens and the earth, it was with the object of securing new territory in which His heavenly empire might be established. But the power of another kingdom, the kingdom of Satan, interfered; and in the fall of man the coming of the kingdom was delayed. For four thousand years it was promised and hoped for, but the kingdom of heaven was not yet on earth.

In the fullness of time, when the King himself came to earth, the message was heard: The kingdom of heaven is at hand, the kingdom of heaven is come to you. He came first as a subject and a servant to show us the spirit that motivates all the subjects of the kingdom—implicit obedience and delight in doing the will of God. In that submission unto death He broke the power of Satan and of sin, showing the wondrous love with which he loved us and set us free for our life of service and obedience. Then when as King He ascended to heaven and took His seat upon the throne, the kingdom could come to earth. By the outpouring of the Holy Spirit, it was set up in the hearts of His people.

And who were the subjects of this kingdom? Jesus said, "Except a man is born again, he cannot see the kingdom of God." Nothing less than the Spirit of God coming in and taking possession of a man could fit him to enter the kingdom or to live as one of its subjects. Jesus also spoke this solemn message: "Blessed are the poor in spirit, for theirs is the kingdom of heaven." To become an heir of the kingdom, nothing was needed but the consciousness and confession of poverty, of having nothing in order that we might possess everything.

The marks of those who truly belong to this kingdom are nothing less than the marks by which the King himself was known on earth: uttermost obedience and love toward God, absolute surrender to His will. And toward man, love—giving oneself to live and die to bring the blessings of the kingdom to all. "The kingdom is not in word but in power"; the kingdom of heaven is above everything the infinite power of eternal life. As the kingdom comes, the power of the Holy Spirit comes also to give the strength to live as members of the kingdom. In each one of whom the kingdom truly takes possession, the prayer "Your kingdom come" becomes the desire of the heart, and everything is subordinate to its extension and manifestation of its glory.

Who then are the children of the kingdom? Jesus spoke this word even of the Jews who rejected the kingdom. God had in His great mercy committed the promise of the kingdom to Israel, and all its children were its heirs. And now our children—born under its influence, destined for its blessing, brought into the fellowship of the church, which is the nursery and training school of the kingdom—are children of the kingdom: "of such is the kingdom of heaven."

What is needed to secure for them the possession of the kingdom to which they have been made heirs? According to our Scripture, it is possible for them to lose it. What is needed above everything is that they be educated and trained under the influence and power of the Christian life, that the blessing that their name implies may become their own personal and everlasting possession.

The next question is, who will train them? Christian parents have this honor. It is primarily and almost exclusively their job and responsibility. These "children of the kingdom" are entrusted to us to keep and to nourish. We have the high commission of leading them on from the place where their title is only a name and a promise to the life of personal possession and full privilege.

Of course, in order for the parent to do this, he must himself live in and for the kingdom of heaven with his whole heart. The atmosphere of the home must be in the spirit of Christ's command: "Seek first the kingdom of God." The child should receive the impression that not only personal blessing but also the interests and extension of God's kingdom are the hope and joy of life. Parents whose citizenship is in heaven will alone be found worthy or fit to train children as heirs of the kingdom.

"My kingdom," Jesus said, "is not of this world. It is from above, from heaven, from God." Being in the world and daily being exposed to its influences, the believer must daily spend time in God's presence in worship and surrender until the anointing is fresh upon him for his work of training his children in the ways of the kingdom.

As long as we are content with just enough "religion" to get by, we must not be surprised if our children remain unsaved. Only in seeking to be filled with the Spirit, to have our whole life, like Christ's, sacrificed for the kingdom, can we count on the effectiveness of our children's spiritual education. To put it simply, the kingdom must come first in the home.

As we have tried to make clear, our offspring are children of the kingdom by virtue of the covenant God has made with families. But we must nurture and love and train them for God alone to ratify their title. From God alone your hope and help comes. Seek it in prayer. Accept it in childlike faith—believe that you have what you ask. Yield yourself to it, denying self, not allowing your own wisdom any say in the guidance of your life or home. Yield yourself to it, keeping your ears open always to the voice of the Holy Spirit, through whom alone the laws and the powers of the kingdom can work.

Above all, remember Jesus! He said, "Suffer the little children to come unto me, for of such is the kingdom of heaven." He is the King; in Him we have the kingdom. Live with Him, by Him, in Him. He loves our children and He looks after them; His presence and love will fill them and us with a holy enthusiasm for the kingdom. Only then will they grow up in the kingdom and for the kingdom. Then we will know the unspeakable joy of having our home, its life and love and training, within the kingdom—of having the kingdom of heaven within our home.

PRAYER OF CONSECRATION

Our Father who art in heaven, yours is the kingdom, and the power, and the glory. Blessed be your name that by your almighty power your kingdom has come to this earth, and will come until the whole earth is filled with your glory. Bless your name for the fact that our little ones are children of the kingdom too. O Father, we look to you for the grace to realize how sacred our calling. Teach us never to separate the words our Lord has joined together—the children and the kingdom. And may all our love and training and influence help to link them inseparably with your kingdom.

You said of the little ones, Lord, "of such is the kingdom." May we be faithful to do our part to be sure they not only bear the name but know in reality that they are truly part of your kingdom here on earth and in heaven. Amen.

CHAPTER 29

A MOTHER'S PERSEVERING PRAYER

"A Canaanite woman from that vicinity came to him, crying out, 'Lord, Son of David, have mercy on me! My daughter is suffering terribly from demon-possession'. . . . Then Jesus answered, 'Woman, you have great faith! Your request is granted.' And her daughter was healed from that very hour."
—Matthew 15:22, 28

In the Old Testament we found God's promises of blessing to be clear and sure on the godly training of children. Neither were His warnings on the neglect of this duty less clear. And in more than one example we saw with what mighty power the warning was realized. In the sons of Aaron and Eli and in the family of David and Solomon, proof was given that the personal righteousness of the father could not save the ungodly child. We found no answer to one of the most solemn questions of a parent's heart: Is there still hope for a child who has chosen the path of sin and seems beyond the reach of a parent's influence?

It is in Christ Jesus that God has revealed how completely the power of sin and Satan has been broken. And it is in Him that God has shown us what is possible for His grace to do. We must seek for the answer in Christ to every question we face as parents. His earthly life revealed what the Father is willing to do for us, and in Him is a parent's hope for a wandering child.

As we study carefully, we will be surprised to find how many of the most precious and encouraging words of Christ have been spoken to parents in reference to their children: "Fear not, only believe"; "All things are possible to him that believes"; "O woman, great is your faith: be it unto you even as you will." Such words, which have countless times been the strength and comfort of the penitent seeking pardon or the believer pleading for some spiritual blessing, are in the first place the parent's property, the blessed assurance that there is no case in which a child now in Satan's power is beyond the reach of the Savior's love and a parent's faith.

Let us look at how wonderfully this is shown in the well-known story of the Syrophenician mother, as we think of her daughter's misery, her prayer's refusal, her faith's perseverance, and her rich reward.

Her daughter's misery: "My daughter is suffering terribly from demon-possession." How many mothers have had a child possessed with an evil spirit far more terrible than the one we read of here? In this case it was a sickness more than a sin; it was the power of Satan in the body more than in the soul. But how many grown children of Christian parents are there who are under the power of Satan, given over to pleasure or worldliness, to self-will or to sin?

May the story cited above encourage parents to believe that however hopeless their case appears, there is One who is mighty to save. Let them come to Him with their need and cry out in prayer, "My [child] is suffering from demon-possession"—or whatever the problem may be. Let them make full confession of their child's lost estate. Beware of excusing their sin by the thought of what is good or lovable about them, or by laying the blame on circumstances or friends. Bring them to Christ and admit that they are lost and under the power of Satan, and that unless they turn away from sin they are on their way to eternal separation from God. Do not try to hide their condition. Do not ask simply that they may be saved and made happy and taken to heaven. Rather, ask that they may turn from the power of Satan unto God, that they may be translated from the power of darkness to the kingdom of God's dear Son. Ask that they may be born again, changed from being the children of the devil and enemies of God to being God's true children and friends. Honor God by fully and clearly confessing their sin and acknowledging His righteous judgment; ask distinctly and definitely for a full salvation.

Her prayer's refusal is the second lesson the Syrophenician woman would teach us. Christ appeared to turn a deaf ear to her prayer. At first He didn't answer her a word. When He did speak, His answer was worse than His silence because it seemed to cut off all hope; He said He was sent only to the lost sheep of Israel (v. 28). A second answer, given as she came nearer, saying, "Lord, have mercy on me," appeared to heap contempt on her misfortune: she was not only a heathen, but a dog (v. 26).

Here is a true picture of what goes on in the heart of many pleading parents. They are reminded of Christ's love and power and begin to pray with urgency. But He doesn't answer, and there is no sign of change on the part of the one who is lost. Still they pray, but it is as if the power of sin grows stronger, and the child only wanders farther away. Conscience begins to accuse parental sin and unworthiness. Others, who seem holier or have more power with God, speak out: how can we expect God to work a miracle for *us*? So the parent settles down to a quiet despondency or a vague hope that tries to shut its eyes to its own despair. The uncertainty as to the salvation of a child is heartrending!

Her faith's perseverance. It is for this virtue that the mother's example is set before us. She refused to be denied. She met silence and argument and seeming contempt alike with one weapon—more prayer and more trust. She had heard of the wondrous Son of Man and His compassion; she saw it in His face; she even heard it in the voice that refused her. She would not believe He could send her away empty. She hoped against hope; she believed against appearances and even against His words; she *believed* and she *triumphed*.

You who are pleading for your prodigal child have her example. And not only this, but a thousand words of promise, a revelation of the Father's will, and the Savior's power and love such as she never had. Let her faith's perseverance put your unbelief to shame. In the face of all appearances and all doubts, let your faith rise and claim the promise of an answer to prayer in the name of Jesus. Yield yourself to the Holy Spirit that He may search out and bring to light everything that is not according to His will, that you might confess it and cast it out. Do not trust the fervency of your desire or the wrestling urgency of your petition, but put your strength in God's promise and faithfulness, in His power and love. Let the soul, in restful, deliberate, confidence in Jesus, praise Him for His promise and power to save. Let nothing shake you from the continuous and persevering prayer of faith—it will be heard.

Her rich reward. The reward she obtained is possible for us too. Not only was her daughter delivered from her trouble but there was something more—a spiritual blessing and our Lord's approval of her faith: "Woman, you have great faith! Your request is granted." Yes, it is in the earnest, believing supplication for a child that the parent's heart is drawn out toward the Lord, where it can learn to know and trust Him and rise to that insight into His love that is so pleasing to Him. Dear mother, if you are pleading for loved ones far from the fold, come nearer, come closer to Jesus. He is able to save them. He waits for your faith to take hold of His strength, to accept their salvation. Do not allow your child to perish because you refuse to come in faith and take time with Him until the assurance is there that you have been heard and your child will come to know and love Him.

PRAYER OF CONSECRATION

Blessed Lord Jesus, like the Syrophenician woman, I too have a child suffering from demon-possession. Like her I come pleading, "Lord, have mercy on me."

I bring before you the sin of my child. You know it all: unconverted and an enemy to you, he has rejected your love, choosing the world and sin. I confess my sin too. You know how bitter the thought is that had my life been less in the world and the flesh, purer and holier, more full of faith and of love and of you, my child might have grown up differently. Lord, in deep sorrow I confess it to you; please do not let my child perish. Have mercy on me and on him.

Blessed Lord, I put my trust in you now. I look in faith to your almighty power and to your promises. The things that are impossible with men are possible with God. I know you hear prayer. Lord, I believe this; help my unbelief. I lay my perishing child at your feet and plead your mercy, grace, and love. I claim deliverance for my child. I will wait at your feet day and night until I see the salvation of my son. For your name's sake, I pray. Amen.

CHAPTER 30

THE HEAVENLY QUALITY OF A LITTLE CHILD

"Therefore, whoever humbles himself like this child is the greatest in the kingdom of heaven. And whoever welcomes a little child like this in my name welcomes me."

—Matthew 18:4–5

The disciples had come to Jesus with the question, "Who is the greatest in the kingdom of heaven?" He had spoken often of the kingdom. To them it suggested the idea of power and glory; they could not help but wonder who would have the highest place. How utterly strange and incomprehensible the answer Jesus gave to their question must have seemed. He called a little child and set him in the midst of them. He told them that as long as they were thinking of who would be greatest, they could not even enter the kingdom; they must first become as little children. And then in the kingdom, the humblest and the most childlike would be the highest. And whoever received one such little child in Jesus' name would be receiving Him. The deeper the empathy with the child-nature, recognizing Jesus and His name in it, the closer and more complete would be the union with himself.

How wonderfully applicable this is to parents! In creating a family, God places a little child with a mother and father. And in that child He opens up the mystery of the kingdom of heaven and the spiritual world. He tells them that if they want to know about heaven and what it is that will fit them for its highest place, they must study the nature of a child. On earth they will find nothing so heaven-like as a little child, and no surer way to the highest enjoyment of heaven than in receiving little children in His name; for in doing this they will receive Him who is Lord of the kingdom.

These are the three lessons we parents must learn. First, *the heavenly quality of a little child.* What is it? Our Savior uses one word: humility. "Whoever *humbles* himself like this child is the greatest in the kingdom of heaven." The greatest one will be the one who thinks the least about being the greatest, because he loses sight of himself in seeking God and His kingdom. The great beauty of childlikeness is the absence of self-consciousness. The true child loses himself in what is around him. The curse of sin is that it makes man his own center; even when he seeks the kingdom of heaven, he is still thinking how he can be greatest in it. In the true child, self does not yet manifest itself; it lives and is at rest outside of itself in the parent. It loves and rejoices in being loved; it is truthful and trustful to all around, showing itself as it is, counting upon others to be what they appear. This naturalness and simplicity of the child, Jesus tells us, is a heavenly quality, the thing in nature closest to the kingdom. And the lesson we need to learn is that there is nothing a parent should seek to preserve and cherish more carefully than this heavenly childlikeness. It is the secret of that beautiful calmness and serenity that is the image of the peace and the rest of heaven.

The spirit of the world is the opposite of this quality; with its rivalry and ambition, its seeking excitement and possessions, it destroys all that is beautiful and heavenly in a child, making way for the demonstration and self-seeking that are its marks. Christian parents who have the means for gratifying taste and pleasure at their disposal are especially in danger of destroying the simplicity and tenderness of the child-life by stimulating desires that are of the world. And so, in the midst of a great deal of Bible-teaching and hymn-singing, the very heart of true religion may be spoiled by the artificial and un-childlike spirit of the home.

Parents should seek to find out what Jesus meant when He spoke so strongly of the need for being childlike as the only path to heaven and heavenly greatness. Value the childlikeness and simplicity of your little one as the beauty of heaven; realize that in its tender susceptibility to impressions, a child is alive to all that surrounds it, whether it is the fostering influence of the heavenly life or the withering effect of a worldly life. Believe that there is a wonderful compatibility between the Holy Spirit, who brings heaven down to us, and the heavenly quality of childhood. Train your children in that holy, happy quietness that keeps the heart open to His workings.

How shall the parent succeed in doing this? Our Lord's words have a second lesson. *If we are to watch over the heavenly quality of our children, we must ourselves be childlike and heavenly-minded.* Christ put a little child in the midst of strong men to teach them. Parents often owe more to the teaching of their children than their children owe to the teaching of their parents. Children lose their childlikeness all too soon because parents have so little of it. The atmosphere of the home should be that of simple, happy, trustful living in the Father's presence. Amid many of the proprieties of religion, the spirit of the world too often reigns. To be great in the kingdom of heaven is all too seldom the object of earnest desire. To be the greatest by being humble and childlike, as Jesus puts it, the least and the servant of all—is hardly a popular goal in life.

Let parents study to be childlike. There are very few studies more difficult, and fewer that will bring a richer reward. The children entrusted to our care have greater worth than we know; even their size, with which we often connect weakness, is what to him who looks at things in the light of God, constitutes their greatest attraction. It is parents living in great simplicity of truth and trust with the Father in heaven that can maintain childlikeness in the child.

The third lesson our Savior would teach us is, *"Whoever welcomes a little child like this in my name welcomes me."* Let us from their birth receive our children in the name of Jesus, in His Spirit, with His appreciation of their simplicity and humility. Let us receive them as those whom He loves and blesses and of whom He says, "of such is the kingdom," to be kept and trained for Him alone. Let us receive them in His name, as sent by Jesus to remind us of His own childlike humility and obedience to the Father. Let us receive them every day in His name, coming as a gift from the Father to draw us closer. Let us receive them and cherish them just as He would receive them, even as He did and blessed them.

It is not asking too much to receive them as we would receive Jesus, for He asks and promises nothing less. He who recognizes and loves the humility, the childlikeness, and the Christlikeness of the little child and on this account receives and treasures him, receives Christ himself. This is the promise. With every child something of heaven and of Christ comes into the home. In many cases this is not observed or enjoyed, and all of heaven is pushed aside by the world. Blessed are they who know to receive the child in Jesus' name.

Jesus comes along with the little one. With the child He sets in their midst, He takes the parents afresh into His training, teaching them how to be great in the kingdom of heaven. He makes their child a blessing to them so that they may be prepared to be a blessing in return. He comes to bless parent and child together and make the home what it was meant to be—the picture, the promise, and the pathway to the Father's home in heaven.

Parents, ask the Lord Jesus to open your minds to take in His divine thoughts about the beauty of our children, to open our eyes to see Him in them, to bring our hearts into perfect harmony with himself so that our little ones every day will be the blessed messengers that lead us to heaven, to Jesus himself.

PRAYER OF CONSECRATION

Open our ears, Lord, to hear what you have to say to us, and our eyes to see what you see. May our hearts keep in tune with you at the sight of every child; and above all, help us to understand and experience how surely and blessedly you fulfill your promise, "Whoever welcomes a little child like this in my name welcomes me."

Lord Jesus, we ask you for a childlike spirit. May the simplicity, the restfulness, the trustfulness, and the truthfulness of the child-nature so dwell in us that in all our relationships the childlikeness of our little ones may not be wasted but cherished and emulated. We want to embrace the truth deeply that we cannot fulfill our parental calling unless we learn to walk with God as a child.

Blessed Lord, thank you for showing us that in receiving a child in your name we receive you. You are our teacher and our helper. Strengthen us, and all parents, for our task. Amen.

CHAPTER 31

LET THE CHILDREN COME TO JESUS

"Jesus said, 'Let the little children come to me, and do not hinder them, for the kingdom of heaven belongs to such as these.' "

—Matthew 19:14

What deep significance there is in this word, "Let the little children come to me." We suffer, allow, or permit that to which we are not naturally inclined, something we would prefer to be otherwise. The mothers had probably heard these words of Jesus (see Matthew 18:3–5) and brought their little ones to be blessed. Jesus saw the disciples rebuking them. They found it so hard to understand and to follow the Master; what could the little children possibly have to do with Him? Jesus hears them, and says, "Do not hinder them; for the kingdom of heaven belongs to such as these." Among His disciples, He loves to have the children gather, for they are nearest the kingdom, the most fitted for it; the kingdom needs them as the teachers of the wise and the great, to show the path by which heaven can be entered.

"Let the little children come to me." The word *let* reminds us how our wisdom cannot understand how the kingdom and the children are fitted for each other. It is no wonder that with such an attitude the church's youthful grace is quenched and the child's religion becomes very much like that of the majority of older people. Let us hear the words of the Master today. Whether you can understand or fully approve, do not forbid or hinder the children from coming to Jesus; bear with it until you see how He can bless them, until His word, "the kingdom . . . belongs to such," has entered your heart and you learn to receive them as He did.

Child-faith is at the very center of God's revelation—coming to Jesus. In His own well-known words, "Come unto me," our Lord spoke of the blessed rest He would give to all who came to Him to exchange their weary burdens for His loving yoke. This simple gospel is just what a child needs. His faith is ready to believe in the unseen One, so kind and loving. His humility finds no difficulty in confessing sin and the need of help. And nothing appears simpler or more natural than that this loving Savior should be obeyed and followed. By instinct he reconciles faith and works and sees at once that trust in Him requires obedience.

But above all, the child takes in what older people often cannot comprehend—faith and salvation is in a living Person—Jesus loving and desiring to be loved, Jesus trusted and obeyed, *Jesus himself*. Oh, that this were true for all! Coming to Jesus in prayer, in surrender, in love, would be the spontaneous exercise of our faith. Let us not hinder but help our children come to Jesus!

I say *do not*, because child-faith can be hindered. The words of Jesus suggest the thought. The child is weaker than the older disciple, is under his influence, and can be held back by him. God has given the spiritual development of the children into the hands of their elders. And the natural responsiveness of the child, his simple faith and sense of love and duty to Jesus, may be severely wounded by the example and the conduct of those around him. The faith of the child is weak and can so easily be discouraged. Christian parents are appointed as guardians to watch over and foster a child's faith. All growth comes from within and depends upon a healthy life. But young growth needs to be preserved from danger and be provided with the sustenance it demands.

Parents are often bitterly disappointed in their children; when they were younger, they felt so deeply and spoke so beautifully. But something has changed. They are no longer "innocent." This is because parents often trust what is a blessed but only a weak beginning. They do not sufficiently watch out for the evil influences to which a young child is so susceptible. They allow the spirit of the world to enter their lives or let the child choose friends who enjoy the company and pleasure of the world, and so the good seed is choked. Or they fail to supply the needed nourishment. There is not, as the child grows, the often speaking of this blessed Jesus, the helping to faith and obedience by the fellowship and example of a warm, living Christianity.

How different the result when coming to Jesus is fostered and encouraged not only in the little ones but also in the maturing boy and girl through the years. We must beware of considering a child's religious impressions of little value. Like all beginnings of life and growth, they may be weak and easily lost, but they are still of infinite value. We must, on the other hand, not overestimate or trust first faith. We must remember that the tender young plant needs a constant watch, and that only in the congenial atmosphere of a home consecrated to the Lord and wholly dedicated to His service can we count on its ripening fruit to eternal life.

We have already suggested what a child's faith needs. Allow the child to come to Jesus and remove every hindrance to his growth. Believe deeply what Jesus says, "the kingdom . . . belongs to such," and allow this heavenly element in the child's nature to show itself and to reach out after the Son of God. In your training, may coming to Jesus to be saved from sin and to have the heart sanctified be your chief goal. Do not come between the child and Jesus; rather, let the child under your leading have free access to Him. Beware of hindering him by distrust or coolness. Let the warmth of your love for Jesus, your holy example of obedience, your teaching and praying—in a word, your whole life— be a daily help to the child to see Jesus, to live with Him, and to long for Him. Jesus Christ is meant to be our everyday friend, our every-hour companion. Let all the wondrous influence you possess in forming your child and fixing his destiny be spent for this one thing: to satisfy the desire of the Savior's heart and to make your child wholly His.

These words of Christ were spoken to the disciples who knew Him and confessed Him as the Son of God. They were sound in the faith, Christ's chosen friends. But they did not understand His thoughts about children; this was too high for them, because the love of childlikeness is one of the highest things in the kingdom. Many a theologian, preacher, and parent is not yet in harmony with Jesus on this. Dear parents, you who have taken the Savior as your only teacher in the revelation of the mysteries of divine love, let Him teach you the unmeasured worth of your children. Learn to see in them what He sees. In His light your care of them will become a blessing to yourself and to them.

PRAYER OF CONSECRATION

Blessed Savior, again we ask you to open our eyes to see in our little ones what you see; to think of them as you do, as belonging to you and to the kingdom. Make this so clear to us that it may become impossible to do otherwise than to lead them to you. Let your claim on them and your love for them be the secret principle that inspires all their education.

And we ask, Lord, for a heavenly wisdom to know how to guide them in coming to you and to help them to abide in you. Teach us to rightly judge a child's impressions, both in their weakness and in their worth, as the seeds of the eternal life. And may our faith in your love for them and in their share in the kingdom be the power by which their young hearts are made strong.

Blessed Lord, you have said, "Come to me." We come now, Lord, and ask for grace to enable us to bring our children too. Grant us your Holy Spirit that day by day and year by year we may train them for you alone and for your glory. Amen.

CHAPTER 32

A FATHER'S TEARS

"Immediately the boy's father exclaimed, 'I do believe; help me overcome my unbelief!'"

—Mark 9:24

When Jesus spoke to the disciples about the mothers who were coming with their little children to Him, He told them to allow the children to come and not to hinder them. In this story He uses a stronger word. When the father of the boy possessed by an evil spirit had told Him that the disciples had not been able to cast out the evil spirit, and Jesus reproved their unbelief, He said, "Bring him to me." The expression is a stronger one, setting forth the same truth. The little ones were quite ready and willing to come to the loving stranger to be blessed. This poor child, at times unconscious or rebellious, had to be brought, whether he knew it or not. There can be no evil spirit so strong, no resistance so desperate, that the parent does not have the liberty and the power to bring his child to Jesus. To every disciple, to every father and mother, in every extremity of sin or need, Christ's voice is heard calling, "Bring the child to me."

If we want to understand what it is to bring to Jesus a child on whom Satan has a hold, we have this clearly set forth in the further discourse of this father with Jesus. When he had told the touching story of how ever since his childhood the boy had been the prey of this terrible trouble and had pleadingly added, "If you can do anything, have compassion on us and help us," Jesus put the responsibility back on the father, saying, "If you can believe, all things are possible." The question was not whether Jesus could and would do it but whether the father could believe. If he did, the healing was sure; if he did not, it could not take place.

"If you can believe, all things are possible." These well-known words put all the blessings of God's mighty saving love at the disposal of faith. By faith we understand both what God has done and what He will do. By faith we see Him who is invisible, in the reality of His almighty power and His love toward us. By faith we receive His word into our heart as a quickening power that works in us the thought and sentiment that was in His heart when He spoke it. By faith our heart, our nature, our life is opened up to give place to God, so as to let Him be and do in us what He pleases. By faith we become fully conscious of the purpose of His will and of his waiting to work it in us. By faith we forsake the visible, our own thoughts and strength, and we look to God to do what He has promised and so give Him the glory. Faith is the exercise of a will that yields itself to God's holy will. "All things are possible to him that believes" because "with God nothing is impossible," and faith is union with God.

In speaking these words to the father of the demon-possessed boy, Jesus gave to us for all time the secret of successful parental training and prayer. He tells us that it is not only the ministers of His gospel, the watchmen and the workers in fields of special danger or difficulty, but every Christian parent who needs to exercise strong faith to secure the salvation of his child. It teaches us that His compassion and power are longing to help us, if we can believe. If not, it is our fault if our children perish.

There are parents who think this is a hard saying. They seek the cause for unconverted and unsaved children in God and not in themselves. How can all the responsibility be thrown on our unbelief? Scripture reveals to us most clearly God's sovereignty;

the final decision of the destiny of each man is in His hands. Scripture reveals as clearly man's responsibility and the all-prevailing power of faith. True humility accepts both statements, bowing to the solemn truth Jesus utters here: if the parent can believe the child can be saved.

Our text tells us how this truth ought to affect us. With tears the father cried, "Lord, I believe, help my unbelief." In the agony of the thought that his unbelief may keep the blessing from his child, in the consciousness of the unbelief still in himself, he bursts into tears and casts himself at Jesus' feet to confess that unbelief and to ask deliverance from it. It is amid these tears of penitence and confession that the faith is exercised to which the victory is given. The devil is cast out, and the child is saved. Christ's blessed and most heart-searching word had done its work; it had revealed the unbelief but also awakened the faith that brought the blessing.

Christ's word must do the same with every parent who pleads for a child's liberation from Satan's power. A father's tears have power. There must be confession and humbling wherever there is to be strong faith. There must be the conviction and confession of the sin of unbelief—that it has been the cause of the blessing being withheld, and that we are guilty by being un-believing. When the disciples asked the Master why they could not cast out this evil spirit, He told them it was because of their unbelief and that unbelief was caused by their lack of prayer and fasting.

Unbelief is not, as many think, a weakness, inexplicable and beyond our power. Unbelief has its reasons: it is an indication of the state of the heart. The worldly man cannot believe. Self-righteous men, proud men, cannot believe. It is only the pure in heart, the humble, the soul that thirsts for God and forsakes all to follow Christ that can be strong in faith. And therefore the first step in the path of an overcoming faith is the confession of its sinfulness.

I have heard parents plead earnestly with God for the conversion of their grown children, secretly fearing that they would not be heard. I saw no sign of confession of parental sin in these. There are parents whose worldliness, whose lack of living faith, whose self-indulgence and neglect in the education of their children have sown the seeds of which they are now reaping the fruit in the departure of their children from God. And yet they wonder why their children are not more faithful. They sometimes pray earnestly for them and try to have the faith, perhaps thinking they have it, that their children will be saved. They may be deceiving themselves. True faith sanctifies. It searches the heart. It confesses the sin of unbelief and all the sins that are its root and strength. It casts itself weeping and helpless at the feet of Jesus. There, and there alone, bowing in weakness, resting on His strength, it obtains the blessing He loves to bestow.

Fathers, you who have sons whom you would fain bring to Jesus to be saved, come and hear the lessons the Lord would teach you. Let these children first send you to Jesus in confession, prayer, and trust; your faith can bring them in. And in yourself and in them you will experience the all-prevailing power and truth of the word: "If you can believe, all things are possible."

PRAYER OF CONSECRATION

Blessed Son of God, look in mercy upon a parent who now comes to you with a child still unconverted and under the power of the Evil One. Lord Jesus, have compassion on us and help us! Let our child be delivered from Satan's power. Make him a child of God! Lord, I have heard your voice, "If you can believe . . ." and it has filled my heart with trembling. I have to confess how little my life has been a life of faith, and how my unbelief has kept the blessing from my child. I have to confess the worldliness and selfishness, the lack of entire surrender and obedience to you that makes a strong faith impossible. I bow in shame at the thought of all the unbelief that even now rises up in me. Lord, I do believe! Help my unbelief.

I do believe, Lord, in your mighty power. I do believe in your infinite love. I do believe in you as my Savior, my Friend, my Covenant Redeemer. I believe, Lord, that you hear me now for this child. I look to your Word and hold it fast. I yield myself to a life of entire surrender to you, to be yours alone. Blessed Lord Jesus, hear me, and save my child. In this confidence I praise your holy name. Amen.

CHAPTER 33

THE SACREDNESS OF MOTHERHOOD

"He will be great in the sight of the Lord. He is never to take wine or other fermented drink, and he will be filled with the Holy Spirit even from birth."

—Luke 1:15

May God grant us His grace to meditate in holy tenderness and reverence on the truth revealed to us here, a truth of unspeakable worth and power to a believing parent: the mother's womb is the workplace of the Holy Spirit. Our Lord taught us that the least in the kingdom of heaven is greater than John the Baptist; if John could be filled with the Holy Spirit from before his birth, how much more, now that Christ is glorified and the Holy Spirit given, can the child of those who have become partakers of full redemption and the indwelling of the Spirit of Christ be filled with the Holy Spirit.

We find here, at the opening of New Testament history, the same truth that came out so strongly in laying the foundations of the covenant with the patriarchs. In preparing and securing servants to do His work, God loves to begin at the very beginning—from before birth, from the moment of conception—to take charge and to sanctify the vessel He is to use for His service. The more clearly we comprehend this part of God's plan with His church, this root-principle of the economy of redemption, the better will we understand the holy privilege and duty of parentage. Especially mothers will be encouraged and strengthened in faith to yield themselves, with all the hopes and joys of motherhood, to be God's chosen vessels for the fulfillment of His purposes and the perfecting of His church.

Let us look first at what Scripture teaches us of the mother in whom the Holy Spirit is to work. Of John's parents it is testified: "Both of them were upright in the sight of God, observing all the Lord's commandments and regulations blamelessly" (Luke 1:6). The God of nature, who in this world of cause and effect has ordered that kind begets kind, is also the God of grace. Though omnipotent and ready to work any miracle He pleases, He carefully observes His own laws; and when He wants a holy child, He seeks holy parents. Throughout Scripture, especially in the New Testament, the blessed indwelling of the Holy Spirit is promised to the obedient. Man must, in obedience to divine command and under the preparatory moving of the Spirit, build the house; then the Holy Spirit and the glory and presence of the Lord take possession and fill it. And so it was of John's parents, who walked in all the commandments and ordinances of the Lord blameless, that he would be born who was to be filled with the Holy Spirit from his mother's womb, and the forerunner of Him who would baptize with the Holy Spirit.

The twofold lesson for every parent, especially every mother, is of deep interest. A righteous and blameless life prepares for and may count on the power of the Holy Spirit in the unborn child. Let expectant mothers who would fulfill their holy calling as ministers of their Lord's purposes study Elizabeth's character: "upright in the sight of God, observing all the Lord's commandments and regulations blamelessly." It is to such a life that God chose us, "that we should be holy and without blame before him in love." It is to such a life Jesus redeemed us: "He reconciled you in his body through death, to present you holy and without blame and without reproof in His sight." Every child of God ought to be and can be blameless and harmless, without mark, in the midst of a perverse generation. Especially every mother should be holy who would offer her body as the temple of the Holy Spirit, that in her the very first beginnings of life may be overshadowed by the Holy Spirit.

Oh, that mothers and fathers understood to what a great degree the spirit of the world and the flesh hinder the influence of the Spirit and weigh upon the child an unholy appetite and passion. Only a life that in deep humility and the faith of Jesus as our sanctification, seeking to walk in obedience and righteousness, and blameless before the Lord, will be accepted and honored by Him. Parents, we have a right to ask, and confidently to expect, the Spirit that is in us to take possession of the life God gives through us. This is the highest and the brightest hope of motherhood: "He will be filled with the Holy Spirit, even from birth."

Let us look now at the angel's message about the child thus conceived and born: "He will be a joy and delight to you, and many will rejoice because of his birth, for he will be great in the sight of the Lord" (Luke 1:14–15). Here we find three marks of a child born under the covering of the Holy Spirit. The parents are to "have joy and delight." How many Christian parents have had reason to say in bitter defeat, "It would have been better if my child had never been born!" If you wish to have divinely given and secured joy and delight in the children that are given you, let the Holy Spirit take possession of them from before their birth. Yours will be the joy of heaven as you see the beauty of the Lord upon them.

If you would have your child blessed and made a blessing, with many to thank God that they knew him, study the story of John's birth in connection with the story of Jesus' birth. It was for Jesus' sake, in the power of the Son of God coming in the flesh, in virtue of his connection with Jesus, that John was filled with the Holy Spirit from his mother's womb. Plead the coming and the birth and the redemption of Jesus on behalf of your child; claim the outpouring of the Spirit upon all flesh and the promise of the Spirit to you and your children. Your faith will be strengthened to perfect confidence that your child may be filled with the Spirit and cause many to rejoice at his birth.

"He will be great in the sight of the Lord" crowns the whole life. A joy to his parents, a blessing to others, and great in the sight of the Lord is the Spirit-born child. Among men he may not make a name, in gifts and talents he may not be great, but he will be great in the sight of Him who sees not as man sees. He will be a vessel God can use for His work, a true way-maker for the coming of the Lord in His kingdom.

Mother, God gives you this picture of Elizabeth and her child of promise with the twofold lesson: live as she did, believe and receive what she did. Your motherhood is in God's sight holier and more blessed than you realize. If you are indeed God's child, you have in everything been placed under the leading and rule of His Holy Spirit.

PRAYER OF CONSECRATION

Blessed Lord, once more you have shown me your way in preparing a seed to serve you. I know you have a deep interest in securing a holy and blameless motherhood. I have seen you training a mother for your service. You fill her heart with the thought of the divine destiny of her child. You stir her faith to the confident expectation of your divine Spirit and blessing on her offspring. You call her in righteousness and blamelessness to her holy work. You in all things teach her that the life she is to bring into the world is a holy gift from you, to be received and borne in a pure and holy vessel.

O great and glorious God, in deep humility your servant bows before you to offer herself to your service. O Father, you who give the Holy Spirit much more surely than earthly fathers give good gifts to their children, fulfill your promise to your child. Let your Holy Spirit dwell in me. If it pleases you to make me the mother of a child, let him be filled with the Spirit from birth. And let my child be born for this one purpose: that he may be great in your sight and a blessing to all around him. Amen.

CHAPTER 34

A MOTHER'S SURRENDER

" 'I am the Lord's servant,' Mary answered. 'May it be to me as you have said.' Then the angel left her."
—Luke 1:38

We have all had opportunity to observe the wonderful oneness between a mother and her child and the extent to which the relationship influences what the child will be. The life the mother imparts to her child is her own life, in the deepest meaning of the term. When God gave His Son to be born of a woman, this law was not violated; the mother He chose for His Son was doubtless all that grace could make her—the perfect vessel through whom He would receive His human nature and disposition.

Just as Jesus is in everything our example, so we may naturally expect that in His mother God gave us a woman to be a special example to mothers. She to whom the heavenly messenger said, "Greetings, you who are highly favored! The Lord is with you. . . . Do not be afraid, Mary, you have found favor with God" (Luke 1:28, 30), and to whom Elizabeth, filled with the Holy Spirit, said, "Blessed are you among women, and blessed is the child you will bear! . . . Blessed is she who has believed that what the Lord has said to her will be accomplished!" (vv. 42, 45), will surely in her words and ways have left an example for every mother who yields herself as Mary did to the Lord. If there were more mothers like Mary, we could confidently say—without forgetting the infinite difference between her child and ours—there would be more children like the child Jesus.

From the human side, what constitutes the most remarkable feature of Mary's motherhood is the childlike simplicity of faith in which she surrendered herself to the divine purpose: " 'I am the Lord's servant. . . . May it be to me as you have said.' " She called herself the Lord's servant, she gave her will and herself up to Him to do what pleased Him, and in quiet trust and expectancy she looked to Him to do what He said.

The same spirit of obedient faith that once equipped Abraham to be the father of the promised seed prepared Mary to become the mother of Him in whom the promise was to be fulfilled. This is not to say that there were never difficulties or questions. In fact, we read, "Mary was greatly troubled at his words and wondered what kind of greeting this might be" (v. 29). When he spoke again, she wasn't afraid to ask, "How will this be . . . since I am a virgin?" (v. 34). But once the angel had spoken to her of the power of the Most High's overshadowing her, she yielded herself to the divine word. She became an example to every mother who would, like her, share the benediction, "Blessed is she who has believed that what the Lord has said to her will be accomplished!" (v. 45). It is the surrender of faith that makes motherhood so blessed: "Blessed are you among women, and blessed is the child you will bear!" (v. 42).

Mary teaches mothers to yield themselves to God for the service of His kingdom, that through them His purpose and glory might be revealed. Though Mary's Son ushered in the kingdom of God, believing parents may raise children to be the stones in the great temple of which Jesus is the cornerstone. The birth of each of our children under God's guardianship is a link in the chain of God's will along with the birth of Isaac and every child of the chosen race down to Christ. Over all the impulses of human love and parenthood there hovers a divine purpose, the carrying out of His plan. Nothing will do more to sanctify the life of a wife and mother than the realization that she is the Lord's servant, that from her the chosen seed is multiplied and from her is born a generation to serve the Lord. Human love can be divinely consecrated; what otherwise appears to be only natural and earthly is elevated to God's will and God's favor.

When we say, "May it be to me as you have said," we are displaying the faith that is in complete submission to God's service. Rather than looking at difficulties or impossibilities, we count upon God to carry out His purpose and to give the grace and the strength for the work to which He has called us. And it is this faith that above everything else equips a woman for the blessed duties of motherhood and that gives her the quiet rest of body and spirit that promotes health and strength.

There is hardly an expectant mother who—as she first becomes aware of her condition—is not at times greatly troubled and asks the question, "How can this be?" And she finds no rest so sure or sweet as to cast her cares on her Lord, letting Him do what seems good. If the God of nature has created her for this calling, and the God of grace has redeemed her to fulfill it in the interests of His kingdom, she surely may trust His power and love to sustain her in her hour of anxiety, doubt, or need.

To fully understand the teaching of Mary's example, there is one trait of her character we must not omit. It is said of her, "Mary treasured up all these things and pondered them in her heart" (Luke 2:19). In the holy quiet of meditation and reflection on what God has said, the spirit of trust is cultivated. It is only as God's words are kept and pondered in the heart that they can quicken and deepen a living faith in Him who spoke them.

Every mother who searches the Scriptures will find words with reference to her sacred calling. When these are truly received and believed, they will fill her heart with confidence and joy. They will teach her to regard everything in relation to the birth of her child as a matter of deep interest to the Father in heaven and of great importance to His kingdom. She will see how all the great and precious promises may be claimed for her child even before it has seen the light of day. She will see how receiving the little one in the name of Jesus holds the promise of Jesus' presence with her and with him. She will find that the training of her child has been provided for in regulations of divine wisdom and love, and that all the grace needed for carrying out these commands is given to each one who, like Mary, will be a servant of the Lord and believe what He has spoken. All the care and fear, the vulnerability and pain in the anticipation of motherhood, all the help and joy and rich reward God has joined with it, is written in the Word; the mother who listens, waits, and believes will, in view of what she both fears and hopes, be able to say, "I am the Lord's servant. . . . May it be to me as you have said." As she waits her time, let quiet retirement open her whole being to the warmth of heaven, let thoughtful, trustful pondering of God's words engage the heart, and she will find how true the word is, "Blessed is she who has believed that what the Lord has said to her will be accomplished!"

What a holy and blessed event the birth of a child becomes when we ponder the birth of Jesus! What a joyous task it becomes in the light of the favor of the Most High God—the means of the fulfillment of His purpose, the promotion of His glory, the experience of His special grace and mercy.

As a mother contemplates these things, she will understand something of the deep meaning of Paul's words, "But women will be saved through childbearing—if they continue in faith, love and holiness with propriety" (1 Timothy 2:15). Just as labor by the sweat of his brow was given to man in his fallen state to be one of his greatest blessings, so the labor of childbearing was given to the woman that through it's discipline the salvation of Christ might more effectually be revealed in her whole character and disposition. It helps, to those who allow it, to form that perfect womanly character that is one of God's most beautiful gifts on earth. It is in this path of loving acceptance of God's appointment and trustful resting in His promise that the word will come true: "Blessed are you among women, and blessed is the child you will bear!"

PRAYER OF CONSECRATION

Grant to your servant the blessed assurance that in this holy calling of motherhood she is indeed your handmaiden, called to the fulfillment of your purposes, set apart for the service of your kingdom. Let this thought teach me to look upon everything connected with the birth of my child as of great interest to my Father. Let it encourage me to cast every fear and burden, every care and pain on Him in whose service they come. Let it sanctify all the hope and joy with which you so wonderfully sweeten the pain of childbirth.

Let it be unto me according to your Word. In childlike faith, Lord, I would take your blessed Word with all its teachings and its promises as my light and strength. In the time of patient waiting and in the hour of deliverance, your Word shall be my strength. Let your Holy Spirit unfold to me the treasures of your Word that I may in my hour of need receive what you have provided for me. And may I be so prepared by it that the child I bear may be trained according to that Word and enter into the full enjoyment of all that it promises to the seed of your people. Amen.

CHAPTER 35

A MOTHER'S THANKSGIVING

"And Mary said: 'My soul glorifies the Lord and my spirit rejoices in God my Savior, for he has been mindful of the humble state of his servant. From now on all generations will call me blessed, for the Mighty One has done great things for me—holy is his name."

—Luke 1:46–49

There is perhaps no moment of such exquisite joy, such unutterable thanksgiving, as when a woman knows herself to be the mother of a living child. Our blessed Lord used this as the type of that wondrous surprise, that strange resurrection joy with which His disciples should find the living One whom they mourned as crucified and dead. "A woman giving birth to a child has pain because her time has come; but when her baby is born she forgets the anguish because of her joy that a child is born into the world" (John 16:21).

A mother will find no more fitting expression for her joy than thanksgiving to Him to whom she owes so much. And for the expression of that thanksgiving she will find in many portions of the Scriptures the most suitable language. A good example of this is Psalm 103: "Praise the LORD, O my soul, and forget not all his benefits—who forgives all your sins and heals all your diseases, who redeems your life from the pit and crowns you with love and compassion, who satisfies your desires with good things so that your youth is renewed like the eagle's." But as the simple summary of all a mother would say, no words will be found more beautiful than those of the mother of our Lord: "And Mary said: 'My soul glorifies the Lord and my spirit rejoices in God my Savior, for he has been mindful of the humble state of his servant.'"

The first week after the birth of the little one is usually a time of weakness, a time when nothing is so needed as quiet and rest for the restoration of nature's exhausted powers. The time is one of wondrous grace, giving the mother opportunity to prepare herself again for her new duties. While household chores and ordinary communication are kept at comparative distance, the Lord would keep His child for a little while in the secret place of His holy presence to encourage and instruct her for the solemn responsibilities awaiting her. And there is nothing that will be more pleasing to her Lord, more refreshing and strengthening for her own life, and a more fitting preparation for blessing to the babe, than the spirit of thanksgiving. The song of praise from the lips of every mother should be repeated day by day: "My soul glorifies the Lord and my spirit rejoices in God my Savior."

It is hardly necessary to remind a mother of all there is to be thankful for. She has but to think of the anxious thoughts and fears she knew before the birth, and her song is, "I sought the LORD, and he answered me; he delivered me from all my fears" (Psalm 34:4). She looks at the precious treasure that has been given her, with all the love and joy it brings into heart and home, and the words come spontaneously, "How can I repay the LORD for all his goodness to me?" (Psalm 116:12). As she looks upon the little one in view of God's purpose and promise, she sees an immortal being, designed to show forth God's glory on earth and sharing that glory in heaven, a jewel in Jesus' crown; and her soul bows in awesome wonder at the thought that the charge of keeping and forming such a treasure should be committed to one so frail. She remembers that through her this child has the promise of the covenant and the zeal of the Spirit; her child is holy because she is one of God's holy ones in Christ.

Mothers, think of all the grace and wisdom and strength provided in Christ to secure to you and your child all that God's love has prepared. Listen to the voice, "My grace is sufficient for you: my strength is made perfect in weakness," and sing again with Mary, "My soul glorifies the Lord and my spirit rejoices in God my Savior." It is not only God's mercies but God himself in whose love they have their value and their continuance; it is God himself in whom Mary, the believer, and the grateful mother is glad and rejoices. True praise uses God's mercies as the steps of the ladder along which it rises, leaving the mercies behind and rejoicing in God alone.

This spirit of thanksgiving in which we rise up to the God who gave these mercies is of greater worth than can be expressed. It elevates and sanctifies the joy, the gift, and the glad possessor, because it lifts all out of the sphere of nature and into the fellowship of the spiritual and the divine. And in this way it is the true preparation for all the work the mother has before her. We saw in Mary's surrender of herself to God that there were combined in it two elements: the surrender to the work she had to perform and the trust that counted on God to do for her what He had promised. In both of these aspects the thanksgiving and joy at the hour of deliverance, if cultivated and maintained, will become guidance and strength.

The labor of bearing a child is but the beginning of that labor of love to which God has appointed and set apart mothers. The whole work of rearing and guarding and training the child is to follow. The spirit of thanksgiving is the best preparation for the altar of consecration. If a mother is indeed to receive grace for the right and successful fulfillment of this new charge, she will need on her part a very distinct consciousness and confession of incapability, a very definite giving up of herself to be the Lord's willing, loving servant for this holy work. As she looks at how much there is to give up or set aside, how much she will have to strive against and overcome to be the mother of a good child, wholly consecrated to God, the thought may come that the sacrifice is too great, that it is impossible to live so entirely given over to God's service. Most of us draw back from being too different from others; we think God will surely bless us and our children even though we are not so holy.

But if such thoughts come, pause and think what God has done. There is the new life entrusted to your care, the love and mercy of God and the promise of more to be poured out. Has the thanksgiving been so shallow, the joy so selfish and earthly that there is a hesitation as to whom our lives belong? I trust not. If the thanksgiving has been genuine, it cannot but lead a mother to say that she will live completely for God so that she may have the grace to train her child to also be entirely the Lord's. "The joy of the Lord is your strength"; a mother's joy is the power for her work. The spirit of thanksgiving leads to the altar of consecration, where mother and child are placed as living sacrifices to be the Lord's alone.

"May it be to me as you have said." This word of faith and trust takes on new meaning after the experience of the first part of its fulfillment. In all the work that awaits the mother in the future, the goodness just experienced teaches her to trust. Let her yield herself willingly not to her work but to her God for His work; she may depend upon His teaching and His help and His strength; they are realities. Let her in the joyful spirit of praise read His Word. As she studies what it says about earthly mothers, she should also note what it says about the Father in heaven and the abounding grace He has undertaken to supply. Her faith will grow strong that her vow of surrender has been accepted, that its fulfillment is possible and certain, and that the joy of a child born into the world is but the beginning of a joy that shall know no end. Let thanksgiving lift the heart to God in praise;

there faith becomes easy. Let faith lift the heart to God too; there thanksgiving becomes natural, and the life of mother and child may become one unceasing song of faith and love, of surrender and obedience, of thanksgiving and praise.

PRAYER OF CONSECRATION

Blessed be the Lord, for He has shown me His marvelous kindness! Bless the Lord, O my soul, and forget not all His benefits! How can I repay the Lord for all his goodness to me?

Father, in this time of frailty but gladness of heart, I draw close to you and praise you for your mercy and love. Here I am, and this precious child you have given me, the witnesses of your great power and goodness; may our lives, all our days, devoted to you, be the sacrifice of thanksgiving we bring.

Hear the prayer of your servant! Let my life, received again as from your hand, indeed become new. In daily communion with my Father, in close fellowship with my Lord Jesus, yielding to the leading and sanctifying of the Holy Spirit, I desire to live only and always for you.

And along with myself, Lord, I offer you my precious child. Let the grace I have asked for equip me to keep this child as your property, a sacred trust from you to nurse and train as your own. Come to me, I pray, in this time of weakness and thanksgiving; in this time of holy quietness let your presence overshadow me and give me the assurance that my prayer is heard, that you have accepted me and my little one to keep forevermore. Amen.

CHAPTER 36

JESUS, THE CHILDREN'S CONFIDENCE

"When the time of their purification according to the Law of Moses had been completed, Joseph and Mary took him to Jerusalem to present him to the Lord (as it is written in the Law of the Lord, 'Every firstborn male is to be consecrated to the Lord'), and to offer a sacrifice in keeping with what is said in the Law of the Lord: 'a pair of doves or two young pigeons.'"
—Luke 2:22–24

According to the law of God in Israel, a newborn child was circumcised at home after eight days. On the fortieth day the mother was to appear in the temple to bring the sacrifice of her purification and to present her child to the Lord. If the child was a firstborn, the presentation had special reference to the firstborn belonging to the Lord, and the child had to be redeemed. The child Jesus was also to be presented to the Lord, being made under the law and like unto His brethren in all things. This was not only that He might experience everything we experience, but also that we might know that every stage and condition has been sanctified by His holy presence and merit. By giving us the Spirit that was in Him during those times, He imparts to us the blessing and the sanctifying grace that flow from fellowship with Him. This truth brings joy and comfort to parents as they bring their little ones to God's house to present them to the Lord.

We will study this presentation of the child Jesus. He was presented to His Father in heaven by His earthly parents. He was a helpless infant but a pleasing sacrifice, a sweet-smelling savor. He came as the firstborn among many brethren, the forerunner through whom our children are made acceptable to the Holy One. He was indeed made like us that we might become like Him; He was made like our children that they might be made like Him.

He was not only Mary's firstborn, but the Father's firstborn among many brethren. Where the firstfruit is holy the whole family is holy. The presentation of the child Jesus to the Father gives us the right to present our children, and makes them acceptable too.

In Israel, the presentation of the child was accompanied with a sacrifice to cleanse away the defilement of sin. Of course, we are defiled too, and need a sacrifice. What mercy that mothers now can look to the blessed Jesus, the great sin offering and atonement (Leviticus 12:6) for their cleansing from all sin, so that they may be accepted and equipped for being true mothers to their children. And what mercy that the children also share in the efficacy of that great sacrifice even before they know what it means. From birth they are holy to the Lord and may receive that Holy Spirit which is the lawful inheritance of the seed of God's believing people.

The object of this presentation of the children in the temple was especially to acknowledge God's claim upon them and to give them back to Him as His property. With what gladness and confidence parents do this when they are reminded of Jesus' presentation in the temple. Let us gladly present them before Him to be wholly His, devoted to His service and glory. Let us place our children beside the holy Child, on His merits, and say, "Father, through your holy child Jesus, I present my child to you to be the Lord's only and forever!"

Be assured that in such a presentation of your child, after the example and in the power and spirit of God's child, there is a rich and sure blessing. Let your faith lay hold of the child-life of

Jesus as belonging to your child, as communicable by the power of the Holy Spirit. And by faith maintain and renew daily the solemn consecration you made of your child before the Lord and witnesses that he belongs to Him who gave him. Rejoice in the divine transaction in which, when you presented your child in the name of Jesus, he *was accepted of the Father as His own.* What we present to God He takes. And what He takes He keeps. Our faith has only to look to God's taking and keeping to know the joyful assurance that the matter is settled between God and us. Let this faith make you strong to train your child for God. And as he is ready to receive it, speak to your child of this faith, of his having been presented to the Father, and of his fellowship in the life and spirit of Him who became Surety for children.

See that your children grow up in His friendship and footsteps. Live as those whose purpose in life is to train their children to be like Jesus. If the challenge is too great, ask the Father whether He desires your child to be trained for Him, and how it should be done. The answer will not be withheld.

We all know that in the economy of grace and in the work of salvation for man, there are always two powers at work: the divine and the human. To the former corresponds faith that looks to God's promise and power; to the latter, works, without which faith cannot be perfected and which obeys and fulfills the will of God. In our study of the teachings of God's Word on the parent's calling, we have found how these two aspects of truth are presented in turn, and how though at first everything appears to depend upon a parent's faith, soon a parent's character and conduct appear to decide all. The two are inseparably interwoven; the more intently we pursue the one line of thought, the clearer the other will become. We will see that the deeper our insight into the indispensable necessity of either, the greater will be our felt need of the other as its complement.

We have again been meditating on the spiritual side of training and speaking less of the practical side. But let me say that there is nothing more intensely practical than an act of real faith. If our presenting a child to the Lord is the act of an intelligent, childlike, heartfelt faith, it will have a mighty influence on our daily treatment of that child. And if it is renewed every day, it will have a lasting effect on our whole relationship to the child as he grows up under our care. As we think of him as God's devoted and accepted property, and as we regard ourselves as trustees to whom he has been committed for keeping and training, as we realize how God would not expect our humanity to take charge of an immortal spirit without providing the grace to do it well, and as we give ourselves, with the child, to a life of consecration and holiness, our faith will be the vital principle ruling all our conduct. Sanctifying our homelife and elevating our spiritual education to what God would have it be, our faith will be the work of His Spirit, transforming through our life each child who has been presented to Him into the likeness of the life of Him who is the firstborn among many brethren.

PRAYER OF CONSECRATION

Eternal God, Father of our Lord Jesus Christ, we come to you with our little one, presenting him to you. We bring him to you that you may look upon him in your great compassion, cleansing from sin and accepting him as your own to be set apart and sealed as holy to the Lord. We do this with full assurance of faith and hope, because your own holy child Jesus was once, as the firstborn, presented in the place and on behalf of all who are brought to you.

Enlighten our understanding to comprehend fully all that your Son's being made a little child implies and secures. Strengthen our faith to comprehend all the fullness of blessing this fact has opened to us. Because our child has been presented to you as Jesus was, may this be the beginning of a likeness that will take possession of his whole life. Give grace to your servants. May we be worthy parents, guardians, and guides of this child who has been given to the Lord. For your name's sake. Amen.

CHAPTER 37

BAPTISM WITH WATER AND WITH THE SPIRIT

"John answered them all, 'I baptize you with water. But one more powerful than I will come, the thongs of whose sandals I am not worthy to untie. He will baptize you with the Holy Spirit and with fire.'"

—Luke 3:16

Man has a twofold nature: the external and visible—the body; and the internal and unseen—the spirit. Sin brought both equally under the power of the curse. In redemption both are made partakers of the glorious liberty of the children of God: "We wait for our adoption, that is, the redemption of our body." The whole man, body and spirit, is to be saved. All God's dealings with us include both sides of our nature. Through the external He seeks to reach the inner man; the inner is renewed that the blessing may pour out and take possession of the outer man.

It is on this ground that we have the twofold baptism of which our text speaks: the baptism with water and the baptism with the Holy Spirit. John the Baptist teaches us the relationship that exists between the two—the insufficiency of the baptism with water in itself and its high value as the pledge and the preparation of what is to come.

First, we note the *faith* that the baptism with water warrants

193

regeneration — cleansing of our nature by the renewal of the Holy Spirit

and demands as a sign and seal of the baptism of the Spirit. It is a *sign* by which God sets forth the working of regeneration, the cleansing of our nature by the renewal of the Holy Spirit. It is also a seal, an assurance that where God has given the water, He most certainly gives the Spirit also. When John came, the coming of Christ was certain too; when John baptized with water, the baptism with the Spirit was sure to come. God gave the one to awaken faith and expectation for the other. *Holy Spirit* So intimate is the connection that our Savior did not hesitate to speak of being "born of water and the Spirit."

God would teach us that what He meant to be one in promise, our faith can make one in reality. As in the whole economy of grace the connecting link between God's promise and His fulfillment is our faith, so it is in this case. The promise of God is not empty words, though our unbelief may make it of none effect. In His purpose, the water and the Spirit are inseparably united: "What God has joined together, let no man put asunder." Let not a parent's unbelief be content without the Spirit. Claim and accept with the most assured confidence the baptism of the Spirit for your child, and in faith believe for it as his divinely secured heritage.

Let's look at the *work* to which the baptism with water calls and pledges us. The story of John teaches us that the Spirit could not be received until the way had been prepared for Him. John knew how little his labors availed until the baptism of the Spirit was given. And yet he labored. He did the double work of preaching repentance of sin and faith in the Lamb of God—a most blessed lesson for the Christian parent.

In some children, the workings of the Spirit begin immediately. In others, they become manifest at very different stages of later growth. But throughout, the Spirit depends on the parent's education along the lines of John's preaching. The child needs to be taught what sin is and what repentance is. He needs to be guided toward the giving up of everything that is not according

! our unbelief may make God's promises none effective!

to the will of God. And he needs to be pointed to Jesus, the Lamb of God, through faith in whom the full flow of the Spirit is to come. Just as in the parent there is to be the harmony of faith and work, so the child must be trained from its earliest youth for the God who asks to be trusted and obeyed. It is through the obedience of faith that the parent and child are prepared for the fulfillment of the promise.

One more lesson from John: The secret of the wondrous union between faith and work is to be found in his deep humility. His preaching was with mighty power. A great revival of religion was taking place. All men were flocking to him; no prophet in Israel had ever preached as he had. And yet he said he wasn't worthy to untie the laces of the Savior's sandals. The more the soul has received of the vision and the fellowship and the power of the Holy One, the deeper the sense of utter unworthiness and absolute dependence; but on the other hand, the deeper the confidence in the truth and power of Him who is seen, the greater the courage for His work. The thought might arise or we might even hear others say that the assured confidence of the Spirit's being given to our children may lead to pride or may lessen exertion on our part to teach them. He who understands what faith is knows the answer. True faith and deep humility are inseparable, because faith is becoming nothing to let God be all. And so true faith and faithful work are no less inseparable, because faith yields itself to God to be used and to work through us. Let it be with the parent as with John; there is nothing that makes us so strong to honor God as when we are bound by the threefold cord of faith, earnest effort, and deep humility.

Christian parent, have you accepted the promise of the Spirit? Hold that promise fast in a living faith. Praise God unceasingly for His gift to your child, even when you do not yet see its fulfillment. In your daily homelife let everything be subordinated to the high destiny for which God has entrusted a child to

faith is becoming nothing to let God be all

195

this child

you: he is to be a vessel filled with His Spirit. Labor earnestly and hopefully with this blessed prospect in view.

As often as these labors reveal to you your inadequacy or your unfaithfulness, look to Him whose servant you are and who has made you the messenger of the Spirit. He will fit you for the work He has given you to do. Jesus has said, "He that believes in me, out of his innermost being shall flow rivers of living water." Believe in Jesus! Try again, and again, and prove the unexhausted fullness of that word. Live your life by the faith of the Son of God. Through you the Spirit will flow out to your child. And each presentation of a child to God will be the glad reminder of the riches of the inheritance awaiting the offspring of God's people.

And you ministers of Christ who may read these lines, seek like John to testify that He who has sent you to baptize with water has said to you that there is One coming after you who will baptize with the Holy Spirit! Let us ask God to make all His servants ministers of the Spirit. May they have grace to speak and act as men who have realized that the Spirit has been given to follow and to seal the message and the work of faith. Especially may they have grace to lead and train both parents and children into the application of that presence of the Holy Spirit in their homelife, through which the family can again take its place as God's first choice for the maintenance and the extension of the kingdom of heaven.

PRAYER OF CONSECRATION

Lord God, teach me, and all believing parents, to believe that wherever the baptism of water is received in your name, you wait to give the baptism of the Spirit also.

Blessed Lord Jesus, I bring my children to you. I claim for them the baptism of the Spirit. By faith I will train them to believe in you that they may by faith come into the personal possession of what I have already received for them. Even before they can believe, I offer myself, that through the influence of my life your blessed Spirit may rest upon them.

Blessed Savior, give me grace to teach them wisely, according to Thy will, preparing them for the ways of the Lord. In my consciousness of my own unworthiness and inadequacy, may this be my one hope and aim: that my children daily live under the rule of your Holy Spirit. Amen.

hope and aim and prayer

that my children daily live under
the rule of your Holy Spirit !

10/2002

Hans-Peter
Anneliese
Karl
Adelheid

CHAPTER 38

A HOME BUILT ON FAITH

*"While Jesus was still speaking, someone came from the house
of Jairus, the synagogue ruler. 'Your daughter is dead,' he said.
'Don't bother the teacher any more.' Hearing this, Jesus said to
Jairus, 'Don't be afraid; just believe, and she will be healed.'"*
—Luke 8:49–50

Don't be afraid; just believe! To thousands that word has
been the messenger of comfort and hope. As they struggled
under the burden of sin, or sought for help in trial or difficulty,
it told them that there was deliverance from fear by believing in
Jesus. Faith can banish fear. And yet how many who have found
a blessing in this word have forgotten that it is a word that especially belongs to parents. In every other use it is but a loan; it
is as parents that we have full right to it. It is Jesus, the Lord of
the home, of parents and children, who speaks: Don't be afraid;
just believe. The word is a double lesson: in our children there is
every reason for fear; in Jesus, every reason for faith.

When we think of the tendency toward evil our children inherit from us, and the mighty power Satan has in this world, we
have good reason to fear. When we see, both in Scripture and in
the world around us, how often the bright promise of childhood
is cut short and the children of a Christian home stray into the
ways of the world and of death, we cannot remind each other

too much of the importance of parental faith, duty, and obedience. *Only believe* must be written on the doorposts of our homes. It must be the motivation for all we are and do for our children.

Remember what God's Word says of faith and its outworking in Hebrews 11. Faith understands; faith offers a better sacrifice; faith pleases God; faith saves the household; faith obeys when it is called; faith receives strength to bear a child; faith offers up the child; faith blesses the children; faith hides the little one; faith saves the firstborn.

Faith is first the spiritual understanding that receives the revelation of God and His purpose. *It hears His voice*; it listens to His call; it believes His promises. Then it is a divine energy, a living principle of action that carries out God's will and inherits all His blessings. It is especially the *parents'* grace we see in Noah, Abraham, Sarah, Jacob, Moses' parents, and Moses. In each case it was faith that made it possible, made it simple and easy as parents to be the channels of a divine blessing to their children.

The power to understand God's purpose with our children, to save our household, to obey God's will in all its rule, to offer our children to God, to bless them and to save them from the destroyer, all depends upon our faith. The living Christ, in whom is our salvation and our strength, is also all we need of blessing and grace for us and our children—it is He who speaks, "Only believe." It is in the knowledge of what He is—it is in His presence—that such a faith is possible and must prevail.

Has He not redeemed our children as well as ourselves from the power of sin? Has He not come to make the covenant of promise, "your God and the God of your house," a brighter and fuller reality than ever it was to Abraham? Has He not secured for us, in the Holy Spirit, a power from on high to fulfill every obligation that rests on us as God's children—this one of keeping our children for Him to whom we belong? Has He not made true all the promises given of old, of God's Spirit upon our offspring, of God's Word not departing from the mouth of our seed's seed forevermore, in that one word on the day of Pentecost, "the promise is to you and to your children"? Can we not count upon Him to give us, and each of our children, just what we need if we only believe?

"Just believe!" Let us take the command literally; faith has never yet been disappointed. Living faith will teach us to see new beauty and worth in our children. Living faith will awaken in us new earnestness and desire in everything to hold and to train them for God alone. Living faith will give its own hopeful and confiding tone to our communion with God for them and our communion with them. The birth of our children, our love for them, our prayer with and for them, our watching out their sins and reproving them, our teaching and training, their lessons and occupations and pleasures—all will be under the inspiring and regulating power of simply *believing*.

It hardly need be said that such a faith life in the home is not possible without the faith life in the heart. We cannot be to our children more than we are to God. It is no longer I that live, but Christ that lives in me; I live by the faith of the Son of God. This must be the language of the father and the mother who would have a home filled with faith. It is not only in moments of special need and prayer or when we are in direct contact with the children that Jesus says, "Just believe," but hour by hour and day by day we must "live by the faith of the Son of God."

Christian parent, this is for you. Each new morning say, "For this day I accept Jesus as my guide for all my duties as a believer and as a parent." Commit simply and fully to Him for every task, every difficulty, every circumstance, every moment, and say confidently, "I know whom I have believed. It is He who has said, 'Just believe'; I am persuaded that what I have committed to Him He is able to keep." This is the secret of a life built on faith and a home built on faith.

PRAYER OF CONSECRATION

Blessed Savior, I thank you for this precious word. I have long heard and understood that it is by faith alone that the sinner is saved. I have begun to understand and experience that, in fact, a Christian is to live entirely by faith, to every hour receive from you the life you desire us to live. Lord, teach me the additional lesson that in the homelife faith is just as much the power of blessing, and that in all my relationships with family members your word is still "Don't be afraid; just believe." Jesus, you are not only the sinner's but also the parent's Friend; in nothing will you delight so much to reveal your saving and sanctifying power as in the family life you have redeemed for the service of your kingdom.

Lord, teach me and all parents how impossible it is to train our children or to be a blessing to them, except as we live the life of faith. Open our eyes to see all that you offer to help our faith and how our love to them, our influence on them, our education and our training, may all be inspired and purified and perfected by the faith in the power of your finished redemption and your abiding presence. Show us how all our weakness and our fears, all the waywardness of our children, and all the wickedness in the world that tempts them, can be fully met by your power and your love, if we only trust you.

Lord Jesus, teach us to know you as the Savior of our children from their birth and through their lives in our care. And let our whole life and conversation with them day by day be by the faith of the Son of God, who loved us and gave himself for us. Amen.

CHAPTER 39

THE VALLEY OF DEATH

*"Meanwhile, all the people were wailing and mourning for her.
'Stop wailing,' Jesus said. 'She is not dead but asleep.'"*

—Luke 8:52

In God's great school of tribulation there are many classes. In the department where God trains parents, there is one passage all fear to enter. And those who are led into it are seen struggling and murmuring. In its darkness, they almost refuse to believe that God is love. Many pass through it with little or no awareness of the divine comfort or cleansing the trial was meant to bring. Others who entered with trepidation can testify that the valley of death was to them the gate of heaven; it was through the death of a little one that they were first led to truly know Jesus. In the case of Jairus with his sleeping daughter, the child's death became the parent's life.

Let us see how Jesus meets the sorrowing parent in this place so feared. The first thing He asks is silence. Jesus comes to the house and finds the crowd making a great disturbance. At once He puts them out and goes in alone, with the parents and three disciples.

One of the things that most effectually hinders the blessing during affliction is too much time spent in fellowship with others, seeking comfort in their sympathy. By clouding the light and the clarity of visible things, the Father draws the soul to himself and to the unseen. "My soul is silent before God; I will hear what the Lord will say to me." He has lessons, often difficult lessons, to teach the parents whose child has been taken away by death. It is when there is true teachableness that looks to God alone and waits on Him that the trial becomes fruitful.

The lessons at the deathbed of a child are not difficult to find. The parent is led to ask, Have I loved my child as the Lord's, or have I looked upon him and treated him as my own possession? Has the spirit of my life and my home been for the education of my child for heaven and holiness? Is there worldliness, selfishness, or sinfulness of which this affliction must remind me? In all I seek for my family, has it indeed been the kingdom first? Affliction can never profit without heart-searching; and heart-searching is impossible except in the holy stillness of soul that is found in separation from others and meeting solely with God.

Let parents beware, in their time of trial, of the dissipation that comes from too much seeing of friends, from seeking and finding comfort in their company. God wants to see us alone; without this He cannot bless or comfort us. Jesus waits to reveal himself in the power of His great salvation as the Surety of the parental covenant—the Redeemer in whom the parent will find all the grace and blessing promised. But He cannot do it except the crowd is put out. He takes His three disciples with Him that His servants may learn in their ministry that by the bedside of a dying or a dead child Jesus wants to be alone with the parents. Even His ministers are to come in only as they come with Him and are appointed by Him.

He is alone with the parents, and now comes the comforting. "Do not weep," He says. Jesus does not condemn weeping; He wept himself. Weeping touches His heart. And yet He says, "Weep not." "Woman, why do you weep?" was His very first word at His resurrection. As the Lamb in the midst of the throne, Jesus leads His redeemed and wipes away all their tears.

Weeping is often self-indulgent, a nursing of our grief. It is the fruit of being too absorbed in ourselves, in the object we mourn, or in the suffering we endure. Weeping often hinders the voice of God being heard, hinders altogether the blessing the affliction was meant to bring. We are so occupied with what we suffer, and God would have us think of the sin with which we made Him suffer. By taking away a child, God means to take us away from ourselves to make room in the heart for himself. Weeping often only fills us with ourselves. God would have us through affliction learn to bear, to love, and to worship His will.

You who mourn, hear the voice of Jesus say, "Weep not." He does not say it without a reason. It is not enough that the tumult of the wailing crowd outside is put away and that there is silence in the room; the tumult of thought and feeling must be hushed too; within the soul there must be silence. At the bidding of Jesus, the gush of tears must be restrained and the heart must turn to Him. Who is this who, with authority, bids us cease our weeping, and what has He to say to justify His injunction?

Jesus leads us from the visible to the invisible; where we see only death, He speaks of life. He comes to rouse us to faith, and to it He reveals himself as the living and life-giving one. "She is not dead but asleep." With these words Jesus draws near to the lifeless form of each little one over whom a mother's breaking heart is weeping. He reminds her that death has been conquered and that the loved one is not truly dead—in the terrible meaning that sin gives the word—but asleep, in the deep and blessed sense that His resurrection gives.

Your little one is not dead. Do not judge by sight alone. There is a better life than the one on this earth—the eternal life in which God dwells. In that life there is a sleep provided for those who are in Christ Jesus, the blessed waiting-time until He comes to gather all His own. As that life and the glory by which it shall be fully manifested is something that has not fully entered the heart to conceive, so is this sleep something that passes knowledge. We know for certain only that it is a most blessed rest—in the bosom of Jesus.

Parents, God's one purpose and desire is to come near to you, to bless you, and to be all you need in this hour. Do not let this time of affliction pass without knowing the experience of Jesus as the parent's Friend, Teacher, Comforter, and Sanctifier. You will one day confess how your loss has become your greatest gain. The presence and power and love of Jesus can more than compensate for the absence and loss of a child. Do not turn away in bitterness and regret, but open your heart and life to Jesus anew.

PRAYER OF CONSECRATION

Blessed Lord, in this hour of deep sorrow I come to you, my Savior and the Savior of my lost child. Condescend, I beseech you, to come with me, my Lord, to the valley of death, where your weeping child waits. Come and be my Comforter and my Teacher. Put out, I pray, the tumult of the crowd, all the sad thoughts and uncontrolled feelings that keep me from hearing your voice. Say to the storm, "Be still!" and let your presence be the great calm. Speak, Lord! I am listening.

Speak of your holy will, and your right to do with your own whatever pleases you. Teach me to say, "Your will be done." Speak, as you see fit, of any sin or wandering from you, of any love of the world, of any lack of love for you and your fellowship, and make me a partaker of your holiness. Teach me, Lord, what you would have me to know through this sorrow.

Comfort your child, Lord. Reveal yourself to me as the resurrection and the life, the Shepherd who has taken His lamb into His bosom. Reveal yourself as my Shepherd, the one who will see to it that the blessing of my affliction is secured. Come nearer to me with your abiding presence. Reveal yourself from now on, more than ever, as our Friend, making yourself at home with us, sanctifying our family life. Come in, Lord Jesus! Come in to this valley of death and reveal yourself to us anew, that we might all be prepared for the day you take each one of us to yourself in glory. Amen.

CHAPTER 40

THE WIDOW'S CHILD

"As he approached the town gate, a dead person was being carried out—the only son of his mother, and she was a widow. And a large crowd from the town was with her. When the Lord saw her, his heart went out to her and he said, 'Don't cry.'"
—Luke 7:12–13

Any attempt to set forth the teaching of Scripture on the education of children would certainly be incomplete if it said nothing about what is always sad and difficult, yet often blessed and successful—a widow's training of her fatherless children. There are few scenes that attract and claim more sympathy, both human and divine. One of the sorest trials that can befall a woman is that of losing her husband, on whom she counted and leaned as her guide and guardian, in whom her life and her love found their joy, to whom she looked as her help and strength in the training of their children. The stricken heart seeks in vain for the object of its affection. The sight of little ones still left her, instead of being a treasure to which her love now clings, at first only adds bitterness to the trial. But rest assured, it is not only the heart of man that is touched by this picture; the heart of God is touched too.

Throughout Scripture, from the repeated commands in the law of Moses down to James' testimony that pure religion teaches us to visit "the fatherless and widows" in their affliction, God never forgets the widow: "A father to the fatherless, a defender of widows, is God in his holy dwelling. The LORD watches over the alien and sustains the fatherless and the widow, but he frustrates the ways of the wicked. Leave your orphans; I will protect their lives. Your widows too can trust in me" (Psalm 68:5; 146:9; Jeremiah 49:11). Such words reveal to us the very heart of God.

In the scene cited in the opening Scripture, how could Jesus fail to show this same compassion? He was the Father's image; God was in Christ. It is as if the picture of the Master's life would be incomplete without the story of the widow of Nain. From what He said of the widow's mite, we know His eye sees a widow's poverty as well as her small (in man's eyes) deed of love. At Nain we see Him as the Comforter of widowed motherhood. Learn what Jesus has to say to a widow weeping over her child. Not only when the tears are those of sorrow over one taken away but also those of anxious love or sad distress at the sight of those still left behind. Jesus said, "Don't cry."

Don't cry, widowed mother, as you look at your little ones and your heart breaks at the thought of their being fatherless. Follow me, as we seek Him who has been anointed "to comfort all who mourn." Weep not, as you wonder how you will train and educate them all alone. Let your soul be silent with Him who came from heaven to the widow to comfort and console.

May the wounded heart not have at least the comfort that the unrestrained flow of tears often brings? Let it be enough that Jesus says to be quiet. All the other parents whose children Jesus blessed came and asked for help. He speaks to the widow without being asked. Her widowhood is sufficient plea: "When the Lord saw her, his heart went out to her and he said, 'Don't cry.'" Jesus is looking at you; do not let your tears keep you from looking and listening to Him. Know that if it could have been, He would have spared you that cup. Now that it has come, He is looking on you in compassion, waiting to comfort and to bless. In tender love but with the voice of authority, Jesus says, "Don't cry."

Jesus was not one who comforted only with words; His words were always followed by deeds. If you will look up to see, He will show you what He will do. To the widowed mother at Nain, He gave back her dead son, who had been to her in place of a husband. His believing people know that though the separation may last awhile, the departed ones who have died in the Lord will be given back to them in glory and forever. Look up to Jesus, the resurrection and the life! They who sleep in Jesus will God bring with Him. The resurrection, the meeting again, the being ever with the Lord, are realities—more real, more mighty than the separation and the sorrow. Look up in faith; it is Jesus who speaks, "Don't cry."

But oh, the desolation that meanwhile fills the heart! The sense of utter frailty and inadequacy to fulfill the charge with the children who still live and who need a father's wise, firm, loving rule! But when Jesus says, "Don't cry," He dries the tears. If Jesus himself were to take the place of the father to these children, would not this make you smile and sing even through the tears? If Jesus would undertake the responsibility of educating your children, of being your adviser and your strength and your assurance of success in your work, would this not be enough to stay the tears? Well, this is what He comes to do. What promises God gave to the widows, Jesus comes now in human tenderness and in the nearness of the Holy Spirit to fulfill. You may trust your fatherless children to Him; He will preserve them; He will, in a divine fullness and power, be the father of the fatherless.

It may be that you, a widowed mother, are reading these words, but they have little meaning for you. Though a Christian, you have yet to learn the full meaning of living by faith, of counting the unseen things surer and clearer than the things of sight; the promise appears to you vague and distant. You hardly dare hope for the reality of Jesus doing this for you. You do not feel as though you are good or holy or believing enough that your children should receive such wonderfully special and divine guidance.

If you would, my sister, learn what Jesus expects of you, that you may with confidence depend upon Him to preserve and bless your children. Your tears will pass away in the sunlight of His love and care. Come and listen. Of a widow He asks but one thing: "Trust me!" This is the message I bring you this day in your anxious widowhood. Trust Jesus!

Let each thought of your departed one lead you to say, "I have Jesus with me—I will trust Him." Let the consciousness of sin and shortcomings, of unfitness for your mother's work, wake the prayer, "Jesus, I will trust you to make me what I should be." Trust Him with your children, with their temporal and their eternal interests.

The life of trust calls for a life of undivided, simple, childlike surrender. Be wholly His and He will prove himself wholly yours. Wait in prayer and supplication, in the silent, restful commitment of every care and fear to Him. Really trust Him; in every prayer make this the chief thing: "I have now entrusted my need to Him; I trust Him with it; I am confident He is mighty and faithful to keep that which I have committed unto Him." They who wholly trust Him, find Him wholly true.

And if the double trial of the widow of Nain should be yours and you mourn the loss not only of a husband but of an only child, remember that Jesus is still the Comforter, though your loss may seem unsupportable. This will be the time when you will find Him doubly precious. You will have grace to say, "My flesh and my heart fail; but God is the strength of my heart and my portion forever."

PRAYER OF CONSECRATION

Blessed Lord Jesus, how shall I praise you for the thoughtful love that would not give us the record of your life without the story of the widow of Nain? Blessed be your name for the revelation of the special place the widow has in your heart, the tenderness of that compassion that drew nigh to her before she knew to look to you!

Lord Jesus, for every widowed mother we pray. Teach each one to come to you with her fatherless children. We bless you that there are thousands of widowed mothers who have proven how wonderfully you can bless the weak and how richly you have blessed their children.

Teach her to put her trust in God. You alone are able and willing to do what we humans dare not expect—what we count impossible—if we honor you by trusting your love. O Savior, help the feeble faith of every widow. Let her desolation and her sorrow and her frailty compel her now to cast herself with her children on you, to depend on you alone. Draw nigh, O compassionate One, and reveal yourself to her. Speak into the depths of her sorrowing, anxious heart your word of comfort: Weep not!

Let your widowed child hear you speaking, see you come to take charge and provide and care for the education of her children. Teach her that her one responsibility is to trust you, in separation from the world, in holy devotion to you, to trust you for more than human guidance—divine guidance and blessing on her children. Let her continue in prayer and supplication in daily communion with you, the unseen One, the true provision for her children. Let her know how truly you are the widow's Friend, the Savior and the Friend of her children. Amen.

goal of parent – guide child to Jesus and to distinct confession of faith in Jesus (HIM)

CHAPTER 41

THE SICK CHILD

spirit of faith – trustful surrender to Jesus

"*Once more he visited Cana in Galilee, where he had turned the water into wine. And there was a certain royal official whose son lay sick at Capernaum.*"

—John 4:46–47

In the wonderful training of the parent through the child, God uses a child's sickness as one of His special means of blessing. And in the parent's training of the child, the sickroom often has been the place where the parent first finds his way to the child's heart, to guide him to Jesus and distinct confession of faith in Him. The beautiful story of the nobleman of Capernaum teaches us how sickness is met, healed, and blessed.

God's great gift to sinful men is Jesus; in His Son He meets our every need. And the one thing God asks of us is a spirit of faith—a trustful surrender to Jesus, allowing Him to be to us all that the Father would have Him to be. And because He has been given to us not only as individuals but as parents to accept blessing on behalf of our children, the one thing that God asks of a parent is faith in Jesus.

As faith in God was the one thing by which the saints of old pleased God, so faith in His Son is the one supreme grace by which the Christian parent can please God and obtain His blessings on his children. All of God's leadings and dealings have this one object and purpose, to make us strong in faith, giving glory to God.

When God allows sickness to come upon the child of one of His believing people, perhaps still young or even an infant, and the parents' hearts are agonized by the sight of his pain or the fear of losing him, the question comes with considerable force, *Why does God permit all this suffering?* The answer Scripture gives is this: for the trial and so for the purifying and the strengthening of faith. God's one purpose with parent and child is to work and increase faith in them. By faith they become capable of receiving the revelation of God's glory and showing it to others; by faith God can dwell in them and work through them. God's one desire is that they should more fully believe in His Son; and our one desire should be to meet the sickness with faith in Jesus.

The one great lesson the story of the nobleman teaches us is the growth and increase of faith that occurs when we encounter Christ. The nobleman's faith begins as a general faith in what he has heard of Christ's compassion and power. When he comes into contact with Him, he believes in Him as a healer. Then it becomes a distinct faith when he believes his child will be healed.

Further, his faith in Jesus the healer is perfected to faith in Him as Savior and Lord: "So he and all his household believed" (v. 53). At first the focus of the nobleman was on his sick son; as he met Jesus and talked with Him, his focus moved to Christ himself. His general faith became specific for the salvation of his whole household.

How is the sickness to be healed? The answer to the second question of our story is very simple: by the power of Jesus. In Matthew, Christ's healing work is presented as the natural result of His atoning work (Isaiah 53; Matthew 8). He took upon himself our human nature, and, having redeemed it, lifted it into the glory of eternal life in heaven.

When on earth, He delighted in healing the sick, something His loving heart could do even when He could not save their souls because of unbelief. In His Word He left the assurance that the prayer of faith would save the sick, because the prayer of a righteous man avails much. A thousand times over He has led His children by His Spirit to apply the promise of His doing whatsoever we ask in faith. This includes receiving healing for a sick child. His great desire in sickness is to educate us into that simple, childlike faith, which though it cannot give account of its assurance to reason, yet through the Holy Spirit has the assurance that its petition is granted, that it has what it asks. Let us claim the life of the beloved sick one for God's glory. The word of Jesus can come to us as real as to the nobleman: "Your son will live."

How is sickness to become a blessing? The Lord Jesus used it as a means of drawing to himself; when it had done this, He took it away that the healing might bind to himself. When the sickness had done its work, the healing perfected what had been begun. The sickness brought the nobleman to Jesus in hope and expectancy; the healing left him a confirmed believer along with his household.

There is a very prevalent opinion that sickness is better than health for true holiness. In the life of Christ and in His work we see no proof of this. Healing obtained directly from Jesus by the prayer of faith, or health received consciously as a gift of redeeming love, both are most wonderful spiritual blessings—bearing in the body the mark of the hand of Jesus. Let each parent whom our Lord leads into this school of sickness realize this, that health, asked for and received in faith, may be a token of even more intimate contact with Jesus than the blessing of the sickbed ever was. As this is understood, we may take courage to make known our desire for health in which there is power for God's glory. The new revelation of the power and love of Jesus will make us, and our household, believers as never before—full of faith and devotion to Him who has so blessed us.

Though God is not the author of sickness, we see that God

uses our sick children as messengers to lead us to Jesus and to faith in Him. These circumstances call us to search the heart and life and home: Have we kept our children wholly for God, trained them for the Lord? Trials make the heart tender and humble, and we are drawn to Jesus. Let us take care lest in all the worry and sorrow the sickness causes, in all the means by which we seek deliverance, in all the fear of losing our child, we miss God's purpose.

Further, let us accept the greater blessing of the healing. The exercise of faith honors God more than anything. Availing ourselves of our privilege, trusting Jesus' word and power, learning to know Him as indeed our helper, experiencing His healing power in distinct answer to our faith—it is this that binds us to Christ. We learn to know Him as the Living One. We have the token of the acceptance of our surrender and our trust. Our home has become the scene for the display of His kingly power. It has sealed afresh the parental covenant. We, and our home, become the Lord's as never before.

PRAYER OF CONSECRATION

Blessed Redeemer, we have learned that sickness has but this one purpose—to draw us to yourself. When you were on earth, the sickness of a child was one of the cords with which the Father drew men to you. And still He takes parents into the sickroom of their little ones that there they may learn to seek and to find you, to wait for and to receive the revelation of your power and love.

Lord Jesus, teach us through all the times of our children's sickness to learn the blessed lesson of coming to you and trusting you. We know that you are watching over us to teach, to comfort, to sanctify, and to heal. Give us the confidence that you are still the same as when you were on earth, mighty to bid the sickness depart and to free us from the power of death. To spare the life of a child for your service, to gladden and sanctify a parent's heart by your grace for the Father's glory, you are still ready to hear the prayer of faith and raise up the child. Grant us this faith that we may honor you and not hinder you from proving with what compassion you hear a parent's cry.

And grant, Lord, when you have graciously heard and given back a child, that the blessed fruit may be that the whole house believes in you as never before. May all see that Jesus is Lord and Master, the beloved Friend of the home. As sickness leads us to seek you, may healing bind us to you and your blessed service. Amen.

that the blessed fruit
may be that the whole
house believes in you

CHAPTER 42

FEED MY LAMBS

"When they had finished eating, Jesus said to Simon Peter, 'Simon son of John, do you truly love me more than these?' 'Yes, Lord,' he said, 'you know that I love you.' Jesus said, 'Feed my lambs.' "

—John 21:15

Peter was a fisherman. After the first miraculous catch of fish, the Lord had said, "Follow me, and I will make you fishers of men." Peter's work on earth was the symbol of his heavenly calling. After the second miraculous catch, in the days preceding the ascension, our Lord no longer called Peter a fisherman but a shepherd. There is deep significance in the change. One great point of difference between the fisherman and the shepherd is that while the former catches what he has neither reared nor fed, seeking only what is full grown and casting back all the little fish, the shepherd directs his special attention to the young and the weak, and on his care for the lambs all his hope depends.

The Fisherman as a type gave no place for the Master to give special charge concerning the children of His church. The shepherd's calling at once suggested the words, "Feed my lambs," and sets forth the deep importance and the blessed reward of giving first place to the little ones of the flock. Peter and Christ's ministers were not to feed only the sheep; the prosperity of the church would especially depend upon their feeding the lambs. What was said to them is very applicable to parents as under-shepherds, who each have their little flock of lambs to keep and rear for the Master. Christ's commission to His church through Peter shows the place the little ones have in His heart and teaches us to think of the weakness, the value, the need, and the hope of our children.

"Feed my lambs," Jesus says, reminding us of the great care necessary for our children. I was once leaving a sheep farm to-ward evening in the company of its master. There were threat-ening clouds; he hurried back to call his son and cry out, "Take great care of the lambs! There is a storm coming." When the Lord was about to ascend the throne, one of His last words was, *Care for the lambs.* The sheep is a weak and helpless animal; how much more the little lamb! It cannot care for itself.

The Master would have every minister and every parent re-alize how utterly dependent the child is on the care of those to whom he is entrusted. He cannot choose the company under whose influence he comes. He knows not yet to choose between good and evil. He knows nothing of the importance of little words or deeds, of forming habits, of sowing good or bad seed, of yielding to the world or to God. All depends upon his sur-roundings; and parents especially have the children in their power. What a solemn responsibility to lead and nourish them carefully, to feed them not with the husks of this world's thoughts and pleasures but with the milk for babes that our Fa-ther has provided, then to lead them on in the green pastures.

"Feed my lambs." The words remind us of the high value of the little ones. In the lambs the shepherd sees the possibilities of the future; as the lambs, so the coming flock. The church of the next generation, the servants with whom in a few years' time Jesus will do His work of converting and saving and blessing men, are the children of today. But how little we have under-stood the admonition to feed the lambs. And He really says more. He says, "Feed *my* lambs," for of such is the kingdom. Not only for what they are to become but also for their childlike simplicity and heavenliness, He loves them and counts them of great worth. For the lesson they continually have to teach grownups, for all the influence they exert in making their parents and elders gentle and humble and trustful, for all the blessings they bring to those who receive them in the name of Jesus, they are to Him of unspeakable worth, the most beautiful part of His flock. Let us try to catch His spirit as He cries, "Feed *my* lambs."

And let us learn to look upon our children in the light in which Jesus looks upon them! Let us pray for the Holy Spirit to make the familiar words *Jesus' lambs* a deep spiritual reality to us, until our hearts tremble at the thought. Our little ones are His lambs; we are daily to feed them as such that they may grow up as the sheep of His pasture.

The children's greatest need is here set before us. Food is the condition for growth. Food is something received from without, to be assimilated and taken into our very life. The body has its food from the visible world. The mind is nourished by the thoughts that enter it. If the spirit feeds, through the mind, on thoughts from the Word of God, it will grow. The little ones cannot seek pasture for themselves; Christ looks to parents to bring to them day by day not a chapter of the Bible simply read over—and in most cases beyond their comprehension—but some thoughts of divine wisdom and love without which the soul cannot possibly grow. The mother concentrates daily on what she will give her child to eat; she ought no less carefully to feed the spirit of each lamb entrusted to her care. The one desire and aim must be to rear him for the Lord. The consecration of the child to the Lord must be the chief goal of her life as a mother.

"Feed my lambs" tells the provision Christ has made for His weaker ones. To whom were the words spoken? To one of whom the question had been asked, "Do you love me?" and who had answered, "Yes, Lord, you know that I love you." Only one who is inspired by love to Jesus can truly take charge of the lambs. This is the test of fitness for the duty of parent and shepherd of the lambs: "Do you love me?"

Let every parent who longs to know how he can obtain the needed qualification for his work answer the question. Let Jesus search your heart until the remembrance of past unfaithfulness brings tears, and the answer comes, "Lord, you know all things, you know that I love you." The blight of so many Christian homes is the lack of a conscious, fervent, and confessed love of Jesus. Nothing influences a child like love; the warmth of a holy love for Jesus will make itself felt. There may be a great deal of practiced religion, of teaching, of praying; it is only love that will conquer.

Love to Jesus will lead us to obey Him very carefully, to walk with Him very closely, and to trust Him very heartily. Love to Jesus will make the desire to please Him very strong and the charge He gives us to keep very precious. Love to Jesus will make our testimony of Him very personal. The food with which we feed the lambs will have the warmth of a divine love about it. Jesus wants parents who love Him, who love Him with their whole heart and strength; this is the provision He has made for His little lambs.

Of the Father it is said, "God is love." Jesus himself is the gift of a love that passes knowledge. His own life and work is one of love—love stronger than death. When the Holy Spirit comes to us, He sheds abroad in our hearts the love of God. Our whole relationship to the divine is to be one of love. And our relationship as parents and children was meant to be one of love. It was to restore this that Jesus came. And He does it by calling parents to love himself and then, receiving the little ones in His name, for His sake, and in the fervor of His love, to take charge of them. He purifies and elevates the love of earth by the love of heaven. The home is consecrated by the light of Jesus' love resting on the children and the power of His love dwelling in the parents.

Christian parents, see and accept your blessed calling; you are the shepherds of divine love to tend and feed the lambs. In His church, the Chief Shepherd has many shepherds to care for the flock, but none who can care for the lambs like the parents. It is to parental love, inspired and sanctified by redeeming love, that Jesus looks for the building up of His church. Let us pray very earnestly that our eyes will be opened to see things as Jesus sees them, to realize by the Holy Spirit what He feels for our little ones, what He expects of us and is ready to do for us in giving us wisdom and strength. When "Feed my lambs" is made the law of a parent's duty, it will inspire gentleness and love; heavenly hope; faithful, watchful care; and an unceasing life of faith in the love and grace and blessing of Jesus on the home!

PRAYER OF CONSECRATION

Blessed Savior, you are the Good Shepherd; I lack nothing. I bless you for the tender love that did not forget the little ones, but did so carefully commit them to the charge of your servant Peter at his installation to the office of shepherd. I bless you for the holy privilege you have bestowed on me to be a parent, with your commission, "Feed my lambs." I bless you with my whole heart for the honor and blessedness of being, in my little sphere, what you are in yours—a gentle, loving shepherd. May my daily experience of the way in which your shepherd-love does its work be a lesson that teaches me how to feed my little flock.

Blessed Master, open my eyes to look upon my children as you do, to regard them always and only in the light of your claim upon them. Let me see what a holy life of fellowship with you, of separation from the world and its spirit, of watchfulness and trust, is needed to do my duty to you and your lambs. Take away every thought of reluctance and fear of difficulty and burden, and let me see how a simple, childlike life with you is the best, the only true training for my parent's work.

And to this end, Lord, fill me with your love. Let love to you be an obedient love, the atmosphere of the home in which my children grow up. You who are the Lamb of God, allow my children to bear the name of God's lambs. Let your holy love in my heart be the inspiring power of all my communion with you and with them. And let me so prove how wonderfully you are my Shepherd and how blessed I am to be their shepherd.

For your name's sake. Amen.

You who are the Lamb of God,
allow my children to bear
the name of God's lambs
11/2/2002

CHAPTER 43

THE HOLY SPIRIT IN THE FAMILY

"The promise is for you and your children and for all who are far off—for all whom the Lord our God will call."

—Acts 2:39

We have not forgotten the frequent use in the Old Testament of the words, "you *and* your house," "you *and* your seed," "you *and* your children," "me *and* my house." These were expressions of the blessed bond that made the whole family one in God's sight and partners in God's covenant and blessing. The expression is found in the New Testament too: "you and your children." Nowhere could it have found a place of deeper significance than here in the book of Acts. On the day of Pentecost, the church of Christ, which had just been born by His resurrection from the dead, received its baptism with the Holy Spirit; the word was heard, "The promise is for you and your children." All the blessings of the new dispensation, the ministration of the Spirit, are at once secured for our children.

The promise is of the Spirit of the glorified Jesus in all His fullness. When we are baptized in the name of the Father, the Son, and the Holy Spirit, we confess our faith in the Holy Trinity. The Holy Spirit, not only as one with the Father and the Son but also as the third person, brings the full and perfect revelation of the divine glory.

All that in the Old Covenant had been promised by God, all that had been manifested and brought near to us of divine grace in Jesus, the Holy Spirit is now to make our very own. Through Him all the promises of God are fulfilled, all grace and salvation in Christ becomes a personal possession and experience. God's Word calls our children the children of promise; it is especially of this promise of the Holy Spirit that they are the heirs. The secret of a godly education is to bring them up in the faith and for the fulfillment of this promise. *In the faith of the promise,* we must learn to look upon the aid and the presence of the Spirit in our daily training of our children as absolutely necessary and indispensable. In all our praying for them and living with them, we must learn to count upon and expect the direct working of the Holy Spirit. So we shall educate them *for the fulfillment of the promise* so that their lives, more than our own, may from their youth be in the power of the Spirit, holy to the Lord.

The promise is to *you* and to your children. The very thought of training children every day in dependence upon the Holy Spirit's presence and with the expectation of His filling them appears to some to be too strange, too lofty, too impractical. The reason for this thinking is simply that these have not yet learned to understand and enjoy the abiding of the Spirit as essential to a true Christian life. The promise of the Spirit is to *you*—realize in your own personal experience that it is only the continual leading of the Spirit that will enable you to live as God intends. Only then can you become ministers of the Spirit to your family.

Oh, that the church of Christ understood the place and the power that the Spirit of God is meant to have in every Christian and in every Christian home! All the complaints about the neglect or the failure of Christian education have their root in this: the Holy Spirit is not expected or accepted as the only sufficient strength of the believer for all God asks of him. As you receive the promise and live and walk in the Spirit, will you receive it for your children too?

As in nature, so in grace, you *and* your children have been linked together for good or for evil. Physically, intellectually, and morally, they are partakers of your life. It may be so spiritually as well. The gift of the Spirit and His gracious workings in you, and in them, does not consist of two separate acts; in and through you He would come to them. Your life, your daily influence, is the channel through which His quickening and sanctifying grace would reach them.

If you are resting content with the thought that you are saved, without seeking to be truly filled with the Spirit—if your life is still more carnal than spiritual, with more of the spirit of the world than of God—do not think it strange if your children grow up unconverted. You are hindering the Holy Spirit. You are breathing day by day into your children the spirit of the world. You are, though it may be unconsciously, effectively using all your influence to train them into man's religion, in harmony with the spirit of the world, instead of true Christianity, in the power of the Holy Spirit sent down from heaven. In spite of your influence, through the faith of others the blessing may reach them, but you have no reason to expect it except as you yield yourselves to be the channel for its conveyance. If nothing else has yet moved us, let us see that for our children's sake nothing less is needed than for us to be filled with the Holy Spirit.

To you is the promise, and to your children. Too many look upon a promise of God as a mere word or thought—something that is without power until they from their side do what is needed to make it effectual. They do not know that the Word of God has in it a living, mighty energy, a divine seed-life, and that if they will but hide and keep it in their hearts, it will produce the faith through which the blessed fulfillment comes. To every parent who reads this, there is a wonderful message: *The promise* of the Holy Spirit in His fullness and His power is to *you and your children*. A promise means that God in His infinite power has bound himself to do what He has said, and that He will most certainly do it for us as soon as we claim it in faith. And the promise here means that the Holy Spirit, with His quickening, sanctifying, and gladdening grace, is ours—waiting to come and to be in our home, in our family life, all that we need to make it holy and happy. And however far our homelife may be from God's ideal, and however impossible it may appear to us that in our circumstances and with our difficulties we shall ever succeed in making it very different, if we will but claim and hold fast the promise in the prayer of faith, God himself will fulfill it. A promise needs two things: the receiver must believe and claim it; the giver must fulfill it and make it true. Let our stand be that of simple, trustful faith in God for ourselves and for our children, counting on the promise: God is faithful to do what He says.

Dear parents, let us open our hearts to take in the promise of God as a divine quickening power; it will itself produce in us the very state of mind that God requires before the fulfillment comes. Let us look upon ourselves as the divinely appointed ministers of the Holy Spirit, to prepare and train our children under His influence from their youth onward, and let us yield ourselves wholly to His guidance and working. To train a child right means training him to be a temple of the Holy Spirit, living ourselves in the power of the Spirit. Let no sense of shortcoming or weakness discourage us; to you is the promise, and to your children. Let us place our lives as parents under the leading of the Holy Spirit. That will mean placing our whole life under His leading, because we can be to our children only what we really are to God. Let the spirit of praise and thanks unceasingly fill us, because God has bestowed the wondrous grace upon us to make our family life the sphere for the special working of His Spirit. Let our unceasing prayer and our confident expectation be that by the power of the Holy Spirit from heaven, our home on earth shall be growing continually nearer to the home in heaven, of which it is meant to be the image and the preparation.

PRAYER OF CONSECRATION

O God, how we bless you for the promise that our home is to be your home, the abode of your Holy Spirit, and that in the happy life of love between parents and children, the Spirit of your divine love is to be the link that binds us together. Glory to your name for the promise of the Holy Spirit to us and to our children!

We come to open wide the doors of our beloved home to you, and to place it with our whole family life at the disposal and under the rule of your Holy Spirit. Let Him take full possession. As parents we desire to claim the fulfillment of the promise. May our love to our children and our desires for them, our daily relationship with them and our influence on them, all be under the continual overshadowing of your Holy Spirit. May our whole life, the invisible atmosphere that surrounds us and that fills our home, be that which your Holy Spirit breathes, holy to the Lord.

We claim the promise for our children. We desire, in simple, childlike faith, to count upon it as a settled thing between you and us that they are the heirs of the promise of the Spirit. Give us grace, O Father, as often as we see in them signs of sin that make us sad, tendencies and dispositions that make us fear, influences around them that signal danger—grace to plead the promise in the full assurance of faith. Our Father, we desire to live each day, guide our homelife, train each child, under the leading of the Holy Spirit. May the holy reverence, the deep, quiet joy, the tender watchfulness, the death to self and the flesh, and the life of faith in Jesus that marks His presence, ever be ours. Amen.

CHAPTER 44

PARENTAL SELF-CULTURE

"You, then, who teach others, do you not teach yourself? You who preach against stealing, do you steal?"
—Romans 2:21

Nothing is more inconsistent and vain than the attempt to teach others without teaching ourselves. Only what the teacher has really mastered and thoroughly made his own can he successfully communicate to others. In the higher sphere of the life-truth that a parent has to impart, it carries far more weight; it is the lesson I first teach myself that I can really teach my child. One of the first laws in the science of home education is that it depends far more on example than precept; what parents are avails more than what they say. There is not one of the great lessons for the child that the parent must not first learn himself. Let us look at some of them.

The great aim of education is to teach the child the responsible use of all the wondrous powers with which God has endowed him, so that when he is grown to adulthood he will be in full use of these gifts. To this end a wise *self-control* is one of the first virtues. As a state cannot prosper if there is no wise, intelligent leader to validate its laws and provide for its needs as they arise, there cannot be happiness in the little empire of the human family unless everything is subject to a ruling power. The child cannot be trained too early to form habits of quiet thoughtfulness in speech and action, giving time and opportunity for the mind and will to hold their rule.

As we have said, this training comes through example far more than through precept. It is the atmosphere of a well-regulated home and the influence of the self-control the parents exhibit that unconsciously make their impression on the child. When parents give in to impulse and temper, perhaps at the very time they are trying to reprove or restrain the child's temper, the effect of the good advice they give is more than neutralized by their own behavior. It is the spirit that influences. The child may never look up and say this, but God's Word on his behalf says, "You, then, who teach others, do you not teach yourself?"

If parents honestly watch themselves, they will discover the causes of their children's failings. Such discovery ought to lead to very earnest confession before God, to a heart-surrender to the teaching of Jesus and the Holy Spirit. We can depend upon divine renewal to fit us for true self-control; and what we by grace teach ourselves will in due time influence our children also.

But self-control must know its object and the path to reach that object. The child finds both in the word we have already repeated often—*obedience.* He must control himself to be able to render obedience to his parents that he in turn may be trained to be obedient to God. Here again, the parent's obedience will be contagious; it will inspire the child. If the parent's position is one of privilege and liberty and command, the child may feel that the burden of obedience is forced upon him, the weaker one.

"Johnny," a father once said to his child, who was hesitating about obeying his father, "whose will must you do, your own or Daddy's?" "Daddy's will," was the reluctant answer, followed immediately by, "But whose will must Daddy do?" The father was able at once to answer, "God's will," and to explain how he considered such obedience his greatest privilege. He could at once take his place by the side of his child as also having to give up his own will. The parent who in all things seeks to do the will of God and can in his prayers, in his children's presence, appeal to God, will find in the witness of such a life a mighty power to inculcate obedience in the child. When, on the contrary, the seeking of our own will marks our relationship with our children, we need not wonder when our education is a failure.

This especially holds true of that great commandment that is the fulfillment of the whole law: "Love your neighbor as yourself." Family life has been ordained of God as the sphere where love can be cultivated. In nothing is our self-control more evident than in loving others, in restraining everything that is selfish or unloving. In the daily life of our children with each other and their companions, we have in miniature the temptations to which they will be exposed later in life. There will be constant opportunity for the exercise of the virtues of gentleness and forbearance, of forgiveness and generosity, of helpfulness and consolation. Principles must not only be taught, but the trouble taken to lead the child to do the right thing easily and lovingly.

Many would like to help the poor, for instance, but do not attempt this undertaking because they don't know how to go about doing it. One of the highest aims of Christian education is to make benevolence the chief object of life. But we know that this can only be attained as parents teach themselves, as well as their children, how to do it.

In the daily life of the family, the parents must seek to show that love is the law of their life. It must be understood that unkind words, harsh judgments, and unloving reports form no part of their conversation. In the relationship with each other, with children, with employees, with friends, and the world around them, love—God's love—must be sought after and manifested. In sympathy with the needy and downcast, in thoughtful consideration of everything by which those who have none to care for them can be helped or comforted, in the loving self-denial exercised for the sake of the poor or the suffering, the example of

Christ and His love must be reduced to practice in daily life. Only in this way can education to a life of love be truly successful.

"You, then, who teach others, do you not teach yourself?" These words, as a searching light, ask whether as parents we are doing the first and most needful thing for our success as teachers of our children: teaching ourselves. If we are to train our children wisely, we must go through a new course of training ourselves. We have to put ourselves in school again, and be teachers and students at once. Of the two scholars whose education has to go on simultaneously, the parent and child, the parent will often find that the child makes more progress. The lessons learned by parents in their attempt to train a child are often of greater importance and difficulty than those the child learns. The first lesson—the one of greatest importance—is learning to be teachable.

Let the parent who begins to see this realize what it means to become a scholar. All schooling requires time and trouble, patience and investment. Teaching that costs nothing is of little value. No one can become even fairly competent to train a child for eternity without making sacrifices. Take time to study God's Word to see what it says about a parent's responsibilities. Study to know man's moral nature and its awesome capacities. Teach yourself to cultivate that nature to its highest potential for God's service; it will be the best preparation for teaching your children successfully. And if you feel a great need for the help of some friend to stimulate and guide, let Jesus be that teacher. He learned obedience that He might show us the way. He came to show us the Father; He will so reveal the Father's love and grace, the fatherly tenderness of our God, that we will be full of joyful assurance that He will not refuse to teach and enable us to be true fathers and mothers to our children. We will understand that to be teachable, obedient, loving children of the heavenly

Father is the surest way to have children who are teachable, obedient, and loving.

PRAYER OF CONSECRATION

Gracious God, I come again to seek the grace I need to be a parent that honors you. Impress upon my heart the fact that I can effectually teach my children only what I have taught myself, and that I can expect only the truth that influences my life to influence theirs.

Dear Lord, I think with shame how often I reprove in them what is only the reflection of what they have seen in me. I confess how much lack there has been of that spirit of childlike love and self-denial, of joyful obedience to you and thoughtful self-sacrifice for others, which would have been to them the highest education. Forgive me what is past, and give me grace in everything to teach myself what I want to teach my children.

Convince my deepest heart that it is as I live as an obedient child toward my Father in heaven that I can teach my children and expect them to be obedient to me. I want a childlike simplicity and obedience to be the atmosphere of my home, the bond that makes us one with our children. As I think of how slow I am at learning, may I be very patient and gentle with my children, and yet full of hope that the lessons I impart to them will have their effect.

Jesus, Master, teach me, that I may be in turn a faithful teacher of my children. Amen.

CHAPTER 45

BAPTIZED INTO CHRIST

"Or don't you know that all of us who were baptized into Christ Jesus were baptized into his death? We were therefore buried with him through baptism into death in order that, just as Christ was raised from the dead through the glory of the Father, we too may live a new life."

—Romans 6:3–4

"And you have been given fullness in Christ, who is the head over every power and authority. In him you were also circumcised, in the putting off of the sinful nature, not with a circumcision done by the hands of men but with the circumcision done by Christ, having been buried with him in baptism and raised with him through your faith in the power of God, who raised him from the dead."

—Colossians 2:10–12

In writing both to the Romans and the Colossians, Paul pleads with believers to live a life of separation from sin and the world—a life of holiness and liberty—and uses their baptism into Christ as his great argument. He unfolds the spiritual meaning of baptism, a union with Christ both in His death and His life, and shows how this is both the obligation and the possibility of a walk like Christ's in newness of life. Baptism is the symbol of the deep spiritual mystery of our perfect oneness with Christ; as it is understood and believed, it is the pledge of an abiding union and the ever-growing likeness to Him.

Parents need to be continually reminded what God meant baptism to be. Without this they cannot educate their children to possess what God intends for them.

In baptism, the death and resurrection of Jesus Christ are symbolized. Scripture teaches that the world in the time of Noah was destroyed and renewed again by a baptism of water. The old nature—humankind in its sinfulness—perished beneath the water. And from it a new and cleansed world emerged; Noah, a believer together with his family, was brought forth again as begotten from the dead. Under Pharaoh's rule, the Israelites were forced to live among the Egyptians without distinction. When Moses finally led them out, however, Pharaoh—representing man's sinful nature—perished in the Red Sea; and out of the waters that were death to Egypt, Israel came forth as God's firstborn to sing the song of redemption.

The Spirit teaches us (1 Peter 3:20; 1 Corinthians 10:2) to regard the waters both of the Flood and the Red Sea as types of baptism and its spiritual meaning. As the Jew, at John's command, went under the waters of baptism, he not only thought of the water's cleansing power, for nothing but death to the old life could allow him to rise in newness of life. Going under the water meant death to the old nature, the putting off of sin in confession and repentance; and coming up out of it meant the profession and the hope of a new life.

John's baptism of water was but a preparation; Jesus Christ alone could give true deliverance from the old nature. But even Christ could not do this until He himself had undergone His own baptism into death. In Him the two elements were united, the old and the new, whereas in the Flood and the Red Sea they were represented by two separate parties. He bore in His own flesh the power of sin—"For we know that our old self was crucified with him so that the body of sin might be done away with, that we should no longer be slaves to sin" (Romans 6:6). He descended into the great deep, where He cried, "Deep calls to deep in the roar of your waterfalls; all your waves and breakers have swept over me" (Psalm 42:7). It was this prospect that made Him say, "But I have a baptism to undergo, and how distressed I am until it is completed!" (Luke 12:50). And again, " 'You don't know what you are asking,' Jesus said to them. 'Can you drink the cup I am going to drink?' " (Matthew 20:22). This was Christ's baptism—a baptism into death.

But this was only half of it. There was also "the coming up out of the water," the entrance to a new life redeemed from destruction. That new life, typified in Noah and Israel, symbolized in John's baptism, had now become a reality. Jesus was raised from the dead in the power of a new, victorious life that can die no more. "We were therefore buried with him through baptism into death, in order that, just as Christ was raised from the dead through the glory of the Father, we too may live a new life." ". . . having been buried with him in baptism and raised with him through your faith in the power of God, who raised him from the dead."

Through the power of the Holy Spirit, baptism is our participation with Jesus Christ in the deepest and most mysterious experiences of His life; as our faith looks to, rests on, claims, and yields itself to the working of God who raised Him, we experience the power of His death and His life working in us; our life becomes conformable to His—that life of His that died and lives forevermore. Reckoning and knowing ourselves to be indeed dead unto sin and alive unto God in Christ, we have the power to walk in newness of life; we are made free from sin and live as the servants of God and of righteousness. As often as the flesh suggests that we must sin, or tells us, with the Colossians, to seek our strength in carnal help and ordinances, God's Word reminds us of our strength: We have been baptized into Christ, into His death and into His life.

Yes, believing parent, your life is the means of grace, the medium appointed and consecrated by God, through which the life of the risen One is to become the life of your child. It is through your life—not your teachings, or prayers, or beliefs, for these are but parts of yourself—but through your life, representing the sum of all you are and of the influences you exercise upon your child, that God would have him inherit the blessings.

It is an urgent call for parents to truly live the life of the baptized, as those who have been made one with Christ in the likeness of His death and resurrection. Let no believing parent say or think that this truth, that this life, is too out of reach for him. If he is a true believer, Christ who died and lives again is his life. He cannot taste the true blessing of the life of faith, cannot praise or honor God in truth, cannot abide fully in Christ, unless he accepts Him as He is.

Live as people who have been baptized into the death of Christ, with the flesh crucified to the world, made free from sin, bearing daily the cross and the dying of the Lord Jesus. Live as those who in baptism have been raised again by faith in the working of God who raised Jesus. Let your faith claim all the power of His resurrection life; all that God worked in Him, He will work in you (Ephesians 1:20, 2:6; 1 Peter 1:21). Let your education of your children be founded in a strong faith in the power of the death and resurrection of Jesus working in and through you to your child.

Lead your child to Jesus, to whom he alone belongs. Lead him to the cross, to take it up and bear it in the love of Jesus. Help him, as sin and self reveal themselves, as the flesh and the world tempt, to practice the self-denial that Jesus links with the cross. Guide him in that path of loving obedience, where true happiness is found. Speak to him of Jesus, the risen One, as a living friend, as the power of his new life. Long before he can understand the theology of it, let his young heart have been won for Jesus and a life like His, devoted to His service.

PRAYER OF CONSECRATION

O God, with my whole heart I thank you for all the blessing and power that is secured to me by my having been baptized into Christ and into His death. Set me apart as a parent so to live as one baptized into Christ's death that first my life and later my teaching may lead my child to experience this blessed life in Christ.

Father, I humbly ask you to deliver me from all ignorance and unbelief concerning this wonderful baptism into Christ's death. Enlighten my understanding, strengthen my will, and enlarge my faith in your mighty working, that my own life may be in the full power and fellowship of the death and the resurrection of Jesus. As crucified to the world, as dead to sin, I yield myself to walk in newness of life with Jesus.

I ask for your grace, that my baptism into the death of Christ through water may be only the preparation for the baptism of your Holy Spirit in full power. May this be my one aim: to have and to teach the power of the cross—it crucifies us to the world and lifts us up unto God. And may the life of Christ be manifested in me and in my home to the glory of your holy name. Amen.

CHAPTER 46

THE HERITAGE OF HOLINESS

"For the unbelieving husband has been sanctified through his wife, and the unbelieving wife has been sanctified through her believing husband. Otherwise your children would be unclean, but as it is, they are holy."

—1 Corinthians 7:14

Let us bless God for this precious statement. There is not a deeper or more distinctly divine word in Scripture than holy; in this statement the whole treasure of holiness, with all that revelation teaches us concerning it, is made the heritage of our children. God's holiness in our children is meant to be; as parents we are the God-ordained links for bringing them into perfect union. To do this, we must first *understand* and *apply* this precious truth.

The revelation of God's holiness was a very gradual one, because it was the opening up of the mystery of the Holy Trinity. First, there was holiness as seen in God, its source and fountain; then in Christ, the Holy One of God, our sanctification; then in the Holy Spirit, as the Spirit of holiness in the church.

Holy. The word expresses a relationship. Whatever was separated unto God and made His property was called holy. The first and simplest thought our faith must take in and fill with spiritual meaning is this: our children belong to God. The very fact of their being born of believing parents make them His in a very special sense. The Lord's redeemed, who love to call themselves His bondservants, have no desire to look upon their children in any other light than wholly and absolutely His.

The word *holy* also suggests a destiny. It is of great importance, as we study the word holy in Scripture, to notice how everything that is called holy had a use and purpose; every holy day and thing, place and person, had its service to fulfill. Let the Christian parent beware of looking upon holiness as a mere means to an end, simply as the way to get safely to heaven. It is infinitely more! Let him realize that his child is God's property, to be used in this world as God directs, to be trained with the one purpose of doing God's will and showing forth His glory. The more clearly this is grasped and made the distinct object of the work of prayer and education, the more quickly will we be able to comprehend its higher meaning and gain the path to the blessing it offers.

"Holy" is the pledge of a divine life-power. Though God himself sometimes uses the word *holy* referring to external relationship or privilege and at other times of spiritual blessing, we must remember that the former always had the latter in view as its aim. Beware of emptying the word of its divine truth and power. If God calls our children holy because of the covenant in which He has claimed them, it is because they are born of a believing parent who is holy in Christ, and therefore they are holy too. The child of true believers, having soul and body under the rule and indwelling of the Holy Spirit, inherits from his parents not only the sinful disposition, but also habits and tendencies and attitudes that the child of unbelievers does not share. These are the true seed-germs of holiness, the working of the Holy Spirit from the mother's womb. Even where it cannot be seen and is very weak, there is a secret heritage of the seed of holiness implanted in the child of the believer. And with this there is given the promise of the divine life and power acquired through the covenant and by birth to holy parentage. There is secured to him the Holy Spirit in whom the holiness of God has reached its full manifestation.

In promising the Holy Spirit to His disciples, our Lord said He would be a river of living water flowing from them to others. The believer has the power to influence those with whom he comes in contact; his faith is to save his household, since the child born of him inherits a blessing in the very life he receives from one who is sanctified by the indwelling of the Holy Spirit. Even in the mother's womb the child can receive the Holy Spirit. Be sure of it, when God calls your child holy, there is the beginning and the pledge of a divine power, even the work of His own Holy Spirit.

The word also describes character. God's holiness is His infinite moral perfection—He hates and destroys evil; He loves and works good. Holiness is the divine energy of which perfect righteousness and infinite love are the revelation. It is identity with himself that God seeks and that He gives. "Be holy; for I am holy." In calling your children holy, God invites you to make them partakers of *His* holiness; without this, holiness is but a name and a shadow. It is the work of the Christian parent to train his children in dispositions and habits, ways of thinking, feeling, and acting that will be in harmony with the fact that they belong to Christ. "Holy in all manner of daily life" is what your children are to be—separated from the world, its spirit and its service; consecrated to God, His Spirit, and His will.

It is as we begin to understand that our children are called holy, separated for God's use, that we will apply it. We will find it a word of power in our dealings with both God and our children. With God it will be the strength of our prayer and faith. We will feel at liberty to claim this for our children, and not be sent away with a mere possibility, a promise without fulfillment, a covenant without a personal experience.

As we plead for the conversion of our children, we can say

with holy boldness: *Have you not said that they are holy?* As we plead still more earnestly that they may not only be saved but truly and fully sanctified, vessels meet for the Master's use, we can confidently cry, *You who have placed the name holy on our children, can you mean anything less than all that your power and love can give?*

Let these thoughts exercise their mighty influence in your dealings with your children. Think of your home and family as His home, the dwelling-place of His holiness. Learn to look upon sin in your children—the spirit of the world or conformity to it—as being at utter variance with a child whom God has set apart for holiness. Mentally write "holiness to the Lord" upon your doorposts. Realize that the first need of a parent whose children would be holy is personal holiness—the indispensable condition for educating holy children. Remember that your own example and conduct are the channels through which the knowledge and the love and the power of holiness are to come to them. Nothing but a life in the holiness of God, a life entirely under the leading of the Spirit of holiness, can fit us for watching over and training the children God has given us.

PRAYER OF CONSECRATION

My meditations on this word of the Holy Spirit have made me feel deeply the need of your divine light, Lord, to teach me what it means when you say that my children are holy. Show me how in this word there is secured to my child all the treasures of sanctification that are prepared in Christ.

The glory that the seraphim praise and worship without ceasing is the glory of your holiness; in it all your attributes have their perfection and their beauty. You have revealed yourself as the Holy One, who makes us holy, your Son as your Holy child, your Spirit as the spirit of holiness. You call your people holy, and now even of our little ones you say, "They are holy."

Your words, O God, are not as man's words. They are not

empty thoughts; they are full of meaning, of life, and of power. Make these words quick and powerful in our hearts that we may understand them, and rejoice in them, and hold fast the infinite blessing they bring us. And grant, Lord, that as we love and train, as we pray and believe for our children, it may all be with this one thing as our motive and aim—that we and they may be separated, holy unto the Lord, realizing and showing forth the glory of your holiness. Amen.

CHAPTER 47

THE REIGN OF LOVE

"Fathers, do not exasperate your children; instead, bring them up in the training and instruction of the Lord."

—Ephesians 6:4

"Fathers, do not embitter your children, or they will become discouraged."

—Colossians 3:21

"Love is patient, love is kind. It does not envy, it does not boast, it is not proud. It is not rude, it is not self-seeking, it is not easily angered, it keeps no record of wrongs."

—1 Corinthians 13:4–5

"Then they can train the younger women to love their husbands and children."

—Titus 2:4

The apostle noticed in the houses he visited how often teaching suffers from a lack of love. He speaks especially to fathers on two occasions here, warning them not to exasperate or embitter their children. His words suggest three thoughts: a child's behavior can be very annoying or irritating; a father often allows himself to be upset or angry by this; the result is often that the child is discouraged. Instead of helping and encouraging his child, he discourages and hinders him. Paul's warning opens up the whole subject of giving reproof or punishment in the right spirit, of the need for patience and wisdom and self-control, of the secret to a parent's rule being a reign of love.

Note again that fathers are especially addressed here. They are obviously expected to take part in the management of the children. There are many fathers who neglect this and put the whole responsibility on the mother. When returning home from the day's work, they don't want to be bothered; the children become a burden and a source of irritation instead of a charge entrusted by the Lord to be met in the spirit of love.

God has complemented the meekness and gentleness of the mother with the firmness and strength of the father; it is as each takes his share in the responsibility, becoming the helper of the other, that the divine blessing can be expected. It is of great importance that, in addition to daily family devotions, there be set times when the father and mother join in reading, conversation, and prayer on the training of their children. One half-hour a week set apart for this purpose, if for only a year, would bring rich rewards. It would draw attention to many important lessons that otherwise may go unnoticed. It would also give opportunity for each parent to seek the aid and counsel of the other.

Peter speaks of parents being heirs together of the gift of life: "Husbands, in the same way be considerate as you live with your wives, and treat them with respect as the weaker partner and as heirs with you of the gracious gift of life, so that nothing will hinder your prayers" (1 Peter 3:7). Let every father accept his calling to take his part in the training of the children.

Fathers, do not exasperate your children. Ordinarily the child has first provoked the father. A child is sometimes wayward, often thoughtless, and by inexperience, ignorant, so that even when he means well he may be the cause of annoyance. It is when the nature of the child is carefully and lovingly taken into account that the parent will be able patiently to bear with him and rightly to train him. It is the privilege and honor of the parent to have this immortal spirit—with all the failings and trials of patience it involves—entrusted to his charge, and to make of the child someone who brings honor and glory to God. Let parents take into account the frailty and the willfulness of their children and not be surprised or taken unawares by what may be trying to their temper and patience; let them see the need for preparing themselves for their work by faith in Him who fits us for every job He gives us to do.

Fathers, do not embitter your children, or they will become discouraged. There is much in some children that provokes; and some fathers, more than others, are easily provoked. Beware above everything of giving in to such provocation; it has been the ruin of many a child. To educate a child is impossible without self-control.

The whole life of the Christian is meant to be one of watchfulness and self-reflection under the guidance of the Holy Spirit. In the home these graces are especially indispensable. The sudden outbreaks of temper in children, the little irritations arising from their disobedience or neglect or mistakes, their quarrels and contrariness, are all occasions for which a father needs the love that is not easily provoked. God meant the rule of the family to be like His own, a reign of law inspired by love.

Do not exasperate your children. However irritating the child may have been, however inclined the father may be to feel angry, he must see to it that he does not provoke the child to anger. One outburst brings about another—an angry father, giving in to his own tendency to overreact, makes an exasperated child.

There is innate in each human heart a sense of the dignity of government and the duty of submission to authority. The calm, quiet assertion of authority helps greatly to bring the offender to the acknowledgment of the justice of his punishment. When the parent, instead of trusting this fact, gives in to anger, sharp reproof, or hasty punishment, the child's temper is stirred, too, and he becomes angry and frustrated. Anger ordinarily stirs up an angry response. The parent is the teacher and example of the child, appointed by God to meet and conquer outbreaks of his temper by the gentle firmness of love. How sad when the very opposite is the case: a father's hasty response inflames the child's anger, and nothing good is accomplished.

In the struggle between good and evil that goes on in the heart of the child, nothing is needed more than encouragement to believe that good will prevail. To build a child up with confidence in what he can accomplish is one of the secrets of success in training. When training a horse, for instance, the utmost care is taken never to overtax the animal or give it a load that might lead to failure; at each difficult juncture, one can see the trainer fully alert with voice and hand to inspire confidence in the horse; the animal must not know that it cannot succeed. Likewise, a child should never be allowed to feel that his immaturity is not taken into account, that his young reasoning is not regarded, that he has not received the empathy, or help, or justice that he expects. This will take a kind of love and thoughtfulness that parents are all too often short of.

More important than anything in the education of a child is the teachable parent. This is one of the reasons why God created the family relationship, and is also one of its chief blessings. Without his knowing it, your child is God's schoolmaster to bring you closer to Christ. Not only the child's tenderness and affection call forth the love of your heart, but also his waywardness and willfulness, because they put you to the test in the school of forbearance and gentleness. See that your displeasure, your reproof, and your punishment are so marked by love that, through it all, the child is ultimately encouraged to good behavior.

But it is not by reproof and punishment, however gently and wisely administered, that parents will keep their children from becoming embittered or discouraged. This is but the negative side; the positive side is of more importance. Prevention is always better than a cure. Cultivate in yourself and in your child that comfort of relationship that minimizes the opportunity for clashes between you. Count upon the wonderful camaraderie that empathy creates. Throw yourself into their interests, entering into their state of mind and viewpoint. Because their nature is as keenly susceptible to empathy *for* others as *from* others, they will easily enter into your spirit and temper and instinctively yield themselves to its influence. And as you seek to maintain the rule of love as a principle of action in all your family life, you will find that the children will catch this spirit and become your helpers in making your home the reflection of the life in which God can guide and train all His children.

PRAYER OF CONSECRATION

Gracious God and Father, the longer we listen to the teaching of your Word on our duties as parents, the more deeply we feel the need of divine grace for doing it right. I come to you humbly confessing my sin. Often misbehavior in my children has been met by a sinful response on my part. I know that this only discourages them. I want to be a parent who models patient love, helping them in their weakness, and by my example encouraging them with the assurance that they, too, can overcome difficulty.

Open my eyes to recognize my holy calling. Give me the deep conviction that nothing but your own Spirit dwelling in me day by day can equip me for training my wayward children in the life of holiness; that nothing but entire surrender to walk with you, to be in everything guided and possessed by your Spirit, can prepare me for my work as a parent.

I pray especially for a baptism of love—of your love. May wisdom and patience be given in meeting each outbreak of frustration in myself and in my children. May the power of a love that enables me to bear and yet to conquer, as well as to inspire confidence in my children, fill my everyday life. Help me, Lord. Amen.

CHAPTER 48

THE NURTURE OF THE LORD

"Fathers, do not exasperate your children; instead, bring them up in the training and instruction of the Lord."

—Ephesians 6:4

We call attention now to the second half of the verse cited in the last chapter: "Bring them up in the training and instruction of the Lord." There is a great difference between instruction and education, between teaching and training. The former is the communication of knowledge, secular or religious; the latter is the development of the faculties, both intellectual and moral, to help the person (in this case, the child) to do and to be what the teaching sets forth. The two words the apostle uses might be translated "*nurture* them in the training and *teaching* of the Lord."

Let us note first the spirit that must pervade the upbringing of our children: "Bring them up in the training and instruction of the Lord." Our children are the Lord's; their whole education must be motivated by this thought. We train them for Him, according to His will, and by His spirit. It is the Lord's own training of which we are to be His ministers to them.

Jesus Christ—the Son of God, our Lord and Master, with His personal presence, His love and rule in heart and home—must be our aim; we must educate our children "unto the Lord." That they may know and love Him, that they may be fitted to obey His will and to serve Him—this must be the goal of our education. And it can be such only as we very earnestly study His will and the rules He has laid down in His Word as we wait for His Spirit to guide and to sanctify us in our efforts.

The two parts that God has joined together in the child may not for a moment be separated. The child's emotional nature, with all its sensitivity and impressionability, is developed first. For the regulation of this, the Creator has endowed the child with two powers—*willing* and *knowing*. Training seeks to influence the will, the power that really makes the person; teaching supplies the knowing by which the willing is to be guided and strengthened. Nurturing in the Lord is to bring up the child that he may be a vessel meet for the Master's use, with every faculty of spirit, soul, and body prepared for doing His will. The training and teaching must work in harmony to secure this objective. The purpose of all instruction and admonition is the forming of the will, which, when completely fashioned, forms the character.

The word *education* is often used of mere instruction. The word *discipline* gives a better idea of what the apostle intended here. The foundation of a useful and happy life will be found in the habit of order and self-control, the ready submission to law, and obedience to duty. The chief objective of education has been attained when not impulse or circumstance, likes or dislikes, but the steady purpose and power of knowing and doing what is right rule the life. Discipline uses the means and exercises the power needed for securing this result. The discipline of the Lord has reference not only to what may be considered religious but also to the child's whole being: spirit, soul, and body.

Whatever contributes to the healthy development of the powers God has bestowed on us is included in the nurture of the Lord. There are what may be called physical virtues, at the foundation of which is order. Order is heaven's first law throughout the immeasurable universe, and in the minutest atoms that the mind can conceive there reigns divine order. Everything submits to a law. If the power of self-control—doing immediately what is seen to be the right thing in its time and place—is not learned, the conversion of a child is to little avail. Parents must prepare the home in which the Spirit of God is to dwell and to find His servants.

The habit of order cultivated in a little child in external things can pass on into his intellectual training and become a mighty power in his moral and spiritual life, calling up virtue: decisiveness of character, firmness of purpose, and strength of will. Submitting to order in external things, the child learns that for everything there is a right way, and that his welfare will be found in entering at once into that way and what it requires.

There are also legal virtues—those distinctly commanded in God's law, such as obedience, truthfulness, justice, and love. Parents cannot too often or too earnestly remind themselves of the power of single acts often repeated, which become habits, and the power of habits to give authority to the principles that underlie the acts. Our moral powers are strengthened by exercise no less than our bodily powers are. Early in life conscience may be so disciplined by godly instruction as to become habitually tender and ready to act. Wise training and the nurturing of a tender conscience cultivate the innate sense of right and wrong, the feeling of guilt and shame after sin is committed, and confidence in the authority of God's Word.

The virtues that belong more distinctly to the New Testament and our great redemption are faith in and love for Jesus, submission to the indwelling and leading of the Holy Spirit, self-denial, holiness, and the humility of a Christlike life. All this does not come automatically or unconsciously; these virtues are developed as a result of training. To be temples of God through the Holy Spirit, to bear His image, and to be fit for the service of the Lord Jesus, must be the aims of the divine nurture by which we bring up our children.

For such training to be successful, it is absolutely necessary that the parent exercise his authority. This does not mean that the parent as the superior asserts his right—it is much more than that. His authority, derived from God, must become an influence that is acquired over time. The parent must prove himself worthy of his position; his command will depend upon the weight of his moral character. To acquire such influence must be a matter of diligent effort and prayer.

All who wish to govern children not by force but by influence, not against their will but by means of it, not in virtue of a position in which they have been placed but in the power of a life that proves them worthy of that position and which secures an instinctive acknowledgment of their authority, must make not only their own duty but especially the nature and the needs of childhood their careful study. Only then can the education of our children become—instead of a series of experiments and failures that teach us wisdom when it is too late to benefit from it—the wise and well-ordered commanding of our household that all may keep the way of the Lord.

True authority has its root and strength in a life in which we do ourselves what we ask our children to do. A life of childlike trust in the Father's love, of submission to His authority, and surrender to His training will make itself felt through the home. It will awaken empathy for our children's needs and failings. And in them it will awaken appreciation for our teachableness of spirit and our quiet restfulness. Finally, the nurturing of our children will be to ourselves and to them truly from the Lord—God's teaching us through them that He may teach them through us.

PRAYER OF CONSECRATION

Dear God and Father, you who have appointed us to bring up our children in your way, we come again asking for wisdom and grace to perform our task. We ask you to show us the dif-

ficulty and the sacredness of our responsibility as well as the nearness and the sufficiency of your help. As we yield ourselves to you, walking with you as your loving, obedient children, we know we will have the power to raise our offspring for you.

We ask for grace to combine the admonition that points out the way with the discipline that trains them to walk in it. We would form our children's character to the order and self-restraint and the submission to law and authority, in which is the secret of happiness. We want to see their bodies and minds developed in such a way that they may be fit and ready instruments to serve you.

We will trust you to show us when we are in danger of falling short. We trust you to accept our childlike desire to obey you and, even though we often fail, we ask you to bless our home. We claim the merit and the presence of Jesus our Lord, and we claim the power of a full salvation for us and for our children. Amen.

CHAPTER 49

HOME RULE

"Now the overseer must be above reproach, the husband of but one wife, temperate, self-controlled, respectable, hospitable, able to teach. . . . He must manage his own family well and see that his children obey him with proper respect. (If anyone does not know how to manage his own family, how can he take care of God's church?) A deacon must be the husband of but one wife and must manage his children and his household well."
—1 Timothy 3:2, 4–5, 12

It is thought provoking that among the qualifications for office bearers in the early church—overseer (bishop or elder) or deacon—a primary consideration was the state of their household. Failure there would have been sufficient to bar them from the office for which personally they might otherwise have appeared fit. It reminds us again how close the link is between parents and children and the unity of the home as a whole. A look at a household suffices to infallibly judge what the parents are, because they make the household what it is. The home is the outgrowth and the expression of their life, the mirror in which often with startling faithfulness their hidden failings are revealed.

Some may be inclined to doubt the truth of this statement. They have so often heard of or known dedicated parents whose children have not turned out well. Is all the blame to be laid on the parents? We have no power to change an evil nature; grace alone can do it. Is it going too far to put the blame for unbelieving or unruly children on the parents and count such a father unfit for holding office in the church because his own household is not what it should be? And yet the Scripture is clear. Paul connects unbelieving and unruly children with failure of home rule and thus unfitness for church rule. He stirs us to search out what causes the training of children by parents, who otherwise appear fit to be leaders in the church, to be robbed of power and blessing.

The first answer is suggested to us by the words of Paul as he argues that failure at home means failure in the church. We may go a step backward and argue that failure in the family is failure in the family head. We have more than once seen that the secret of home rule is self-rule, first being ourselves what we want our children to be. The wonderful power of the will with which man has been endowed was meant to make him in the first place his own master.

And yet how many Christian parents are there to whom self-control in daily life is quite foreign? It is not the thought of God's will or the rule of their own will that guides and decides their conduct, but in conversation and in action, in likes and dislikes, they are led by their feelings of the moment. Because they trust that they are God's children and that Christ's blood pardons their sins, and that their prayers will be heard, they hope for the salvation of their children. And yet their mode of education is setting up the most effectual barrier against God's grace. Pleasing themselves, allowing their inclination or temper to be the rule of language and conduct, they contradict their profession of being the servants of God's will.

All Christian parents must learn that quiet self-reflection and self-control and a calmness of soul that seeks to be guided by God's Spirit, is one of the first conditions of success in our own spiritual life and in the influence we wish to make on our children. "In quietness and confidence is our strength," the Word says. Nowhere will the unconscious but strong influence of this restfulness be so felt as in the family.

But there may be other causes for parental failure. A Christian parent may not be lacking in self-control, but may still be guilty of neglect in the area of his exercise of authority. With some this may come from complete ignorance as to the importance of the parent's role in the life of the child. They may never have thought seriously of the extent to which the souls and wills and characters of the children are in their hands. They may pray earnestly at times that their children may be saved, not knowing that it is of more importance to pray daily that they themselves be fitted to guide their children in the right paths.

With others, neglect of duty rests on wrong principles thoughtlessly adopted. They admire a strong will, for instance, and in the waywardness or self-assertion of a child they often see nothing but cause for amusement or admiration. They wish to see their child grow up a strong, bold character, able to do and dare; they would not for anything weaken his will. They don't know that a wayward will is really a curse; and that a will that masters itself by obedience is the truly strong will. No wonder these children later on will be disobedient or unruly.

Sometimes neglect of parental responsibility comes from simple weakness and sloth. Parents may admit what is their duty, but they feel it is so hard; it takes so much time and thought. It is so trying to their love to punish or to refuse the child and, under cover of tenderheartedness, the authority with which they have been entrusted of God is neglected and abused. Let parents take time and thought to realize: to rule a child is as distinctly God's command as to love and care for him. The interests of parent and child demand it, and the time and labor spent in cultivating it will be richly rewarded.

Unfortunately there are still a few parents in whom none of the causes of failure mentioned are true—they do rule themselves and they do seek to rule their children—and yet they have failed. Could there be a *lack of true faith and consecration*? Some children are easily ruled, simply because they are of a pliable nature; there are others of a nervous temperament or wayward disposition who defy control. But we must maintain, "the things that are impossible with men are possible with God." To work with God means to walk closely with Him. The soul that is wholly given over to Him and seeks undividedly to do His will is given the power of faith to hold fast the covenant, living in the assurance that God himself will do the work.

Try simple, childlike heart-searching to see if there has been any desire for worldly honor in our aims for our children; the spirit of the world is the most secret but most certain hindrance to true faith. The surrender of ourselves and our children—not only to God's mercy to save but also to God's will to rule and to use—must be complete and unreserved. We will find God to be our ally, our covenant-helper in training the children, and with Him on our side we must prevail. To have power with Him in prayer is the surest guarantee of victory with the child.

Parents, the work entrusted to us is more serious than we know. A precious human being, so delicate, so wonderfully made, though marred by sin already and exposed to its power, is of inconceivable worth. When we see the enormity of the task of taking charge of an immortal soul, to train a will for God and eternity, we naturally shrink from it. But we cannot. If we are parents, the duty is laid upon us and we cannot deny it. But, thank God, there is promised sufficient grace.

If we will only give up our home and our life to God for Him to come in and rule, He will take possession of it, and you, and by the gentle influence of His Holy Spirit bow the will of each to himself. The discipline that our ruling of the children brings will be the best preparation for our ruling in God's house: "Whoever would be chief among you let him be your servant."

If for the sake of serving God in our homes we deny ourselves to acquire more influence and power to rule our children,

He will count us worthy of influence and power with our fellow-men in His church. Faithfulness in home rule will give power to take care of the church of God, and will be, as it was with Abraham, the secret of admission to the counsel of Him who rules the world.

PRAYER OF CONSECRATION

Lord God, we worship you as the Ruler of the universe. Righteousness and judgment are the foundation of your throne. You are gracious and full of compassion, slow to anger, and of great mercy. Your kingdom rules over all, and is the fountain of all blessing and good.

I know, Lord, that you are pleased with every home that reflects your heavenly rule. You have given to parents the power and authority to rule their children. You have promised to give us all the wisdom and strength we need for maintaining our authority and ruling our children well.

We confess with shame how often this holy trust of ruling in your name has been neglected and abused. We ask your forgiveness. Deliver us from all that hinders us from fulfilling our duty in this area. We desire to take it up as a lifework done in your strength. Help us to rule ourselves so that we are better equipped to rule in our home. Please teach us and help us in this endeavor.

Lord Jesus, we do indeed yield our homes and our children, our lives and all our powers, completely over to you. You are more than able to keep what we commit to you. Guard our home and keep it as your sacred dwelling place, where our children and we serve you in righteousness and love, in peace, and in great joy. Amen.

CHAPTER 50

CHILDREN AND THE SCRIPTURES

"I have been reminded of your sincere faith, which first lived in your grandmother Lois and in your mother Eunice and, I am persuaded, now lives in you also."

—2 Timothy 1:5

"But as for you, continue in what you have learned and have become convinced of, because you know those from whom you learned it, and how from infancy you have known the holy Scriptures, which are able to make you wise for salvation through faith in Christ Jesus."

—2 Timothy 3:14–15

In these two passages we catch a glimpse of the importance of the relationship of parents and grandparents to their children and the passing on of godly example and faith to future generations. Timothy's strong faith was owing to the example of his mother and grandmother. The believing parent is Scripture's messenger, and Scripture is the vehicle for the communication of his faith.

God has ordained that through the Holy Spirit dwelling in His saints His Word is brought to sinners. The same Spirit that empowers the Word empowers the child of God to share it; in the combined action of the two the word is made a blessing to others. One of the highest honors God has bestowed on the believing parent is the joy of ministering the Word of God to his children. The added dimension of personal testimony and experience is used of God to awaken a child's faith. Living faith is contagious; the life of the Spirit breathes in it and makes it powerful to bless, convict, and convert.

Teach your child to first of all believe *the Word of God.* There is nothing more pleasing to God than faith. Faith is the soul's surrender to God, to hear what He says, to take what He gives, to receive what He works, to be entirely at His disposal. Faith in God begins with faith in His Word, and there is no habit a parent can cultivate in a child of deeper importance than that of a trustful acceptance of all that God has said.

In an age of doubt and questioning, *teach your child to* accept *what he cannot understand*—even what appears mysterious and contrary to reason—because God who is wise and great has said it. Teach him to believe in His love, in the gift of His Son, and in the life through Him as realities that become a part of us as our faith simply trusts the Word and is assured of what it says. Teach him day by day to look upon every promise, every truth in the Word as food for faith meant to make his life stronger. A child is naturally trustful; guide him to trust the Word that never fails.

Teach your child to know *the Word of God.* Faith depends upon knowledge. Timothy *knew* the sacred writings were able to make him wise unto salvation. If the grace of God is to save us, it must teach us. It is wisdom from above; we must love God with the mind as well as the heart. Parents must work to give children a clear and intelligent understanding of the great truths of salvation that God has revealed. We cannot entrust this work to the school or the church; it is astounding how vague the knowledge obtained in these institutions can be.

Family worship should be so ordered as to be truly helpful in gaining knowledge of God's Word. Try always to make clear at what stage in the history of the kingdom and in the progress of revelation the word you have read was given. Make the effort to fix in the mind not only the truths and the history of the

Bible, but especially the memory of God's own words. But don't be content with your child's having memorized and said his text at the time appointed; he may forget it as soon as he has said it. Seek rather to have some of these words, by frequent repetition, so rooted in his mind that nothing can erase them. Teach your child to know the Book itself—to be at home in it, to feel at ease with it.

Teach your child to love *God's Word.* This is more difficult than teaching him to believe it and to know it. Often the assent of faith and an interest in the knowledge of Scripture has very little to do with love. The first requisite, of course, is that we parents love the Word. Love and joy go together; what I love I want to possess. Reverence and respect for God's Word, the earnest study of it, and the desire to be guided by it—these are good, but they do not necessarily breathe that bright spirit of delight that says to God, "O how I love your law!"

And yet it is love to which a child's heart is especially vulnerable. Childhood is the age of feeling and impression; the child can be won before he can give a reason for his hope. And a parent's holy, tender love for the Word of God will be the surest means of inspiring the child's love. Let this be a particular matter of desire and prayer and of careful study: so to guide the child in his familiarity with the Bible that he may not only like it for its stories and its study, but truly and heartily love it as his Father's Word.

Teach your child to obey *the Word of God.* God connects all believing, knowing, and loving with *doing;* obedience is God's test of uprightness and reality. Teach your child to make what the Father has said his standard of conduct. Let him also observe that you do the same. In ordinary Christian teaching, children get the idea that God's commandments are difficult and burdensome. To think that obedience to Him can be wholehearted and ultimately bring happiness is not a common concept. And yet this kind of thinking is the only one that will take hold of the heart of a child.

The Bible must not be as a law that continually holds us in

check, keeping us from what we would like to do, always demanding what is difficult. With children it is imperative to take up an entirely different position. As the Father's redeemed children of His covenant and kingdom, we must say, along with His Son, "I delight to do your will, O God; your law is in my heart." It is His covenant promise to work this in our children and in us. If in Christ Jesus we enter into the blessed life of the liberty of God's children, our young ones will learn from us that it is impossible to read the Father's Word and not do it.

Although the practice of a family devotional time is found in most Christian homes every day, there is often little power or blessing with it. This is because the average Christian parent looks more to his personal reading for profit and nourishment. How unfortunate! The daily gathering of the family around the Word of God is meant to be a time of spiritual refreshment and nourishment, and should be a happy—even fun—event for the children. Think of the care that is taken to have a proper meal for breakfast so that each child is nourished for the day of study and play ahead. The same care should be taken for his spiritual nourishment and strength. Each one should leave the house with a sense of the blessing of God and of his parents upon his day.

Beware, too, of the hurry that allows barely time enough for the hasty reading of a chapter. Family worship that is a dead ritual hardens children into the habit of careless dealing with the Word of God—and with God himself. A few moments devoted to a quiet, loving calling of attention to what God says and to making personal application, encouraging the children to take and keep the Word, can be the beginning of great blessing in the life of each child.

God's Word is your child's heritage from the Father in heaven. You are commissioned to lead him into the knowledge and the love and the possession of its treasures. Make it a matter of fervent prayer that you may wisely and rightly do it. Let the Word dwell in you richly in all wisdom. Jesus said that if we will abide in His Word, His words will abide in us.

Let your life be one of wholehearted faith that delights in doing God's work. Such faith will pass on to your children. The quiet confidence that comes from trusting and believing in God's Word is a power that will be felt by your children. And if you feel that you do not know how to teach the Word to them, to make it interesting or exciting for them, take heart—God will make it come alive to them if you are faithful to read it and live it. Pray and believe for the Holy Spirit's working; He will make His Word the seed of faith in your children.

PRAYER OF CONSECRATION

Gracious God, we ask you to give us a very deep sense of the blessedness of this part of our work as parents, to bring your holy Word to our children. May they have the same privilege as Timothy had—from earliest youth to have the example of mother and grandmother as his interpreter of the Scriptures. May a deep, full, and very joyous faith in your blessed Word be the result of our reading and teaching together as a family. Remind us that their hearts are claimed by you already to be filled with your words as seeds of faith—a forerunner of your great salvation.

We ask you for the grace and wisdom and faithfulness to patiently present your Word day by day as the bread of life. May our family worship be a season of true communion with you, a time of preparation for the trials and joys of the day ahead. We yield ourselves to the supremacy and power of your holy Word; let it so abide in us that our life may be an example of your holy life and light. Let us be so full of faith and love and obedience to the Word that our dear children learn from a very young age to love and believe and obey it too.

Father, forgive us where we have fallen short of this most important task. Help us to keep the time spent in your Word with our children sacred and profitable. Amen.

CHAPTER 51

BELIEVING CHILDREN

"Appoint elders in every town, as I directed you. An elder must be blameless, the husband of but one wife, a man whose children believe and are not open to the charge of being wild and disobedient."

—Titus 1:5–6

God expects the children of believers to be believers too. There is nothing so honoring or pleasing to God as faith and trust in Him; nothing so opens the way for His blessing and love to flow in and take possession of us than that we believe Him. The very object and purpose of God in the institution of the parental covenant is that believing parents should have believing children. They are the children of the promise; God and His grace are theirs. But a promise has no value except it is believed. Parents who truly believe will understand that it is their privilege and their duty to train their children to believe.

On the day of Pentecost, with the outpouring of the Holy Spirit, Peter announced that the foundation principle of God's covenant with Abraham was to remain unchanged and that children were to be regarded as heirs of the promise. As ordained by God, the household was still to be the channel for the transmission of the blessing of the Spirit. Faith was not to be solely a personal thing but an act that embraced the household and then flowed out to enclose every family member.

It is in harmony with this that we so often find in the book of Acts mention made of the "household." Cornelius feared God with his house. Lydia was baptized, and her household. To the jailer at Philippi, Paul said, "Believe, and you will be saved, and your house, and he was baptized, and all his, immediately," and he rejoiced greatly with all his house, having believed in God. Crispus, the ruler of the synagogue at Corinth, believed in the Lord with all his house.

In the epistles of Paul we find four times the use of the expression, "the church in your house"; he does not say the church assembling in your house, but the church that is in your house, evidently referring to the circle of believers constituting the family. Though in these cases no express mention is made of children, the principle of the unity of the family, on which the idea of a household rests, assures us that the children were included. It is so clear to Paul, in fact, that believing parents ought to have believing children that when such is not the case he regards it as a matter of blame, as a sure index that there is something wrong on the part of the parents, that their own faith and life have not been what it should be. They are at once debarred from holding any place of honor or influence in the church of Christ. When the father, as the ruler of the church in the home, has not taught his children to believe, he is unfit for taking care of the house of God. Children who believe are to be found naturally in the home whose life is truly one of faith. Let us try to grasp the lesson God would teach us.

Even children can be believers. Trustfulness, the power of simply believing what is told, of resting on what love has promised, is one of the most beautiful traits of true childlikeness. It is this wonderful power of a child's heart, of which the parent avails himself every day and that often fills him with such gladness, that must be guided heavenward and led to cling to God and His Word, to Jesus and His love. There is nothing more natural to children than to believe; it is through a parent's faith that the Holy Spirit loves to take possession of the child's faith and make it the living link to a living Savior. As the child grows, the faith grows—a deep and hidden root of life that even amid temporary trial or disappointment holds onto the blessed Savior.

God expects our children to grow up believers. We ought to expect it too. The very nature of faith in God seeks to think as He thinks, to count upon Him for what with man and nature is impossible, to make His promise and His power the measure of its hope. Let us realize that God's wonderful promise to our children is meant to take possession of us and fill us with a sense of His holy power waiting to fulfill it in their lives. The confidence that our children will grow up true believers—something higher than the confidence that they will eventually be saved—will exercise its influence on us and on them. For us it is a daily call to a life of holiness and consecration; to our children it is an expectation of God's working in their lives to make them all He wants them to be.

One proof that our children are believers will be their conduct. Faith is made perfect by works. Like every other function of life, it can grow and become strong only by action. A life of faith is always a life of obedience. And a child's faith proves itself in obedience to his parents. Children who are allowed to be unruly and disobedient and self-willed will lose their childlike faith.

Faith is surrender. I yield myself entirely to the influence of the news I hear, of the promise I receive, of the person I trust. Faith in Jesus is surrender to Him, to be influenced, ruled, mastered by Him. Faith in Jesus is surrender to His will. Parents must seek to lead the little ones' simple faith in Jesus to this surrender. May the learned obedience to parents become unquestioning obedience to Jesus.

If our children do not believe, we must seek the cause in ourselves. God's promise is sure and His provision is perfect. It may be that the spirit of the world so prevails in our heart and home that while the Sunday lessons teach the children faith in Jesus, the weekday life trains them to faith in the world, to a surrender to its spirit and rule. Or it may be that while we are enthusiastically engaged in Christian work, there is little true spirituality in our lives or in our homes. Only the love and power of holiness can make Christianity a reality. Religion can become an occupation like any other, and when it is nothing more than this, the presence of Jesus cannot be felt by our children. Even when there has been a true striving after following the Lord and serving Him, there may have been failure in devoting ourselves to the task of training our children; we have left this work to others, and neglected the self-denial and the study needed to equip ourselves for the work of ruling them well and of guiding them in the ways of the Lord. Let us seek honestly and earnestly to discover the reason for our failure, to solve the dilemma: We are believers, we have a faithful God, and yet we have children who do not believe, and show it by their behavior.

God calls us to heart-searching, confession, and a return to our responsibility. Even if we have children who believe but who do not have the power and devotion we would wish, let us turn to God in humble new surrender. Our homelife needs the power of a true consecration. The light of the Savior's love and the joy of His presence emanating from us—this is what our homes need for the successful education of our children.

Each new step in the path of entire separation unto God and of greater faith in His abiding and keeping presence must make itself felt in the family. If there are circumstances and influences that appear to make it impossible, let us remember what faith can do: it can bring Almighty God and His power into the situation. We may not obtain at once what we ask. But we can know the assurance of God's working in us and in our children in His time and in His way.

Full surrender in our homes will transform them into what God would have, including believing, obedient children. Let us ponder and remember well: There is no power so mighty as that of a quiet, restful faith that believes that God has given what we have asked and has taken charge of what we have entrusted to Him. Parents who believe with their whole heart and strength and life will have children who believe, and who show it by their behavior.

PRAYER OF CONSECRATION

Blessed Lord God, the God of the families of Israel, we thank you for each message that reminds us of what you would have our children to be, as the proof of the reality of our faith in your Word and our life in your love. Stamp deep in our hearts the truth that in every believing home you seek for and fully expect to find believing children. As trees of your planting, they are yours and shall bear fruit for you.

If you do not find this fruit, reveal to us the cause. Whether it is unbelief or worldliness, the lack of ruling well or the lack of living well, reveal, we pray, any sin, that it may be confessed and forsaken. Especially show us if the problem is our lack of an undivided consecration to your will—with its consequent lack of a full assurance and experience of your presence.

Blessed Lord Jesus, it was your presence so near and loving and mighty to bless that drew so many parents to trust you when you were here on earth. And it is your presence with us now that will strengthen our faith and give us children that believe. We place our home open before you. Come in and have full rule and reign. Be our joy and gladness every day. We have yielded ourselves to live each moment under your rule; we have believed in your acceptance of our sacrifice to keep us abiding in you. Give us the wisdom and sweetness, the faith and the power to be a blessing in our home. And give us children who believe, children you can use in your kingdom for your glory. Amen.

CHAPTER 52

THE CHILDREN GOD HAS GIVEN

"And again, 'I will put my trust in him.' And again he says,
'Here am I, and the children God has given me.' "

—Hebrews 2:13

These words were originally used by the prophet Isaiah: "Behold, I and the children whom the Lord has given me are for signs and for wonders in Israel." The prophet and his family were to be God's witnesses to certain great truths that God did not want His people to forget. In the epistle to the Hebrews, these words of the Holy Spirit are put into the mouth of Christ; He was confessing His relation to those whom He is not ashamed to call His brethren. They are words of the believing parent who presents himself with his children before the Lord in the consciousness of that wonderful unity of the Spirit in which the family is one before God.

As we draw our meditations to a close, these words invite us to gather up all that the Word has taught us of the purpose and the promise of our God, of the work of love committed to us, and the abounding hope in which we may look to the fulfillment of what God has led us to expect.

"Here am I, and the children God has given me." Let this be the language of a deep and living faith as we think of the wonderful ground of our unity. I am one with my children by virtue of God's eternal purpose when He created man and instituted the family. He meant the parent to bear children in his own likeness, to impart his own life and spirit to them, to have one life with them. When sin entered, the promise and the covenant were given to restore the blessing that had been lost; again, the parent was to receive for the child by faith and communicate to him the grace God had bestowed. In virtue of that promise, I am one with my children and my children are one with me in the enjoyment of the love and the life that comes through Jesus.

In the same faith as Isaiah, I present myself before the Father. He has given me my children. They are to be inseparably and eternally one with me. God has given them to me in the power of the complete redemption found in His Son, with the sure and full promise of His Holy Spirit for them and for me. God has given them to me to keep and to train for Him, and then present before Him as mine as well as His.

In this faith I want day by day to look upon my little flock as one with me in the possession of all the promises and blessings of the covenant, of all that the love of my God can give. When for a time it may appear as if they are not growing up as one with me in Christ, my faith will hold firm to God's promises. And even when the thought of past sin and neglect in my training causes me to fear lest my guilt is the cause of their being unconverted, I will still look to the blood sprinkled on the doorposts of my home, and say, "Here am I, and the children God has given me."

In Jesus Christ nothing avails but faith working by love. When spoken in loving faith, the promise becomes the inspiration for the work God has committed to us. The bond between a parent and child is a double one—there is the unity of life and the unity of love. Two lives become one in faith and purpose. The love that is ours by nature cares for and rears and nurtures the child. It is this love that God takes possession of and sanctifies for His service. And it is this love that becomes the strength for the difficult times.

Love is equal to self-surrender and self-sacrifice. It gives itself away to its beloved. True love has no rest apart from perfect union with the beloved; all it has must be shared together. And God calls His redeemed ones who are parents to so love their children—to identify themselves with them, to seek and claim their salvation as much as their own. And as the Spirit of Christ takes possession of the heart, the parent accepts the call. In the unity of a love that cannot think of itself without the children, that is ready to sacrifice everything to make them partakers of God's blessing, the parent learns to say with a new meaning, "Here am I, and the children God has given me."

I am the giver of their physical life, the framer of their character, the keeper of their souls, the trustee of their eternal destiny. I was first blessed that I may bless them, first taught how my Jesus loved me and gave himself for me that I may know how to love and how to give myself for them. I, having experienced how patient and gentle and tender He is with my ignorance and slowness and willfulness, am set apart not to think of my ease or comfort but in the meekness and gentleness and long-suffering of Christ to watch over and to bear with their weaknesses. I am made one with these children, that in the power of love I may be willing to study what they need and the way I may best influence them; to train myself for the work of ruling well, and training them to self-rule. I will walk in the obedience and liberty of a loving child of God, guiding them in the happy art of an obedience to authority that is always free—freedom that is submissive to the law.

The consciousness grows upon me that, in the unity of love, what I am the children will be also. And the more tenderly my love to them is stirred up, the more I feel the need to be wholly and only the Lord's, entirely given up to the love that loves and makes itself one with me. This will fill me with a love from which selfishness shall be banished, giving itself in a divine strength t live for the children that God has given me.

When faith and love have spoken, hope will have courage take up the song, and in full assurance to say, "We are insepara bly and eternally one." Hope is the child of faith and love. Faith is its strength for waiting and watching, love its strength for willing and working. Hope ever looks forward. It sees even in this life, when things are dark, the unseen God coming through the clouds to fulfill His Word. It sings the song of victory when others see nothing but defeat. Amid all the struggles through which it may see a beloved child passing, amid all the trials of faith and patience, hope speaks, "In His Word do I hope. I will hope continually, and will praise Him more and more." With a positive tone, hope inspires hopefulness in children when they are discouraged. Hope is the morning star of the home. It looks forward to each one of the family circle being not only saved but also sanctified, fit for the Master's service here on earth.

And as often as it looks for the blessed hope, the appearing of our Lord Jesus, and the glory that is to follow, hope rejoices in the full assurance of an unbroken family circle in heaven. It even now trembles with joy as it thinks of the privilege that waits when the Son has presented himself with His brethren in glory, saying to God, "Here am I, with the children you have given me." Because it is then that the parent will say also, "Here am I, with the children you have given me." May God teach us to rejoice in this hope! May the God of hope fill your hearts with joy and peace in believing, that ye may abound in hope in the power of the Holy Spirit.

Beloved fellow-believers, whom God has honored to be parents, let us seek to have the spirit of these words breathe through our homelife. It is God who has given us the children; it is He who regards them as one with us in His covenant and blessing and teaches us to regard them so. His love calls and fits for a life of self-sacrifice and unselfishness; His grace will accept and give success to our efforts to be perfectly one with our children in the power of faith and love and hope.

PRAYER OF CONSECRATION

Our gracious Father, we do thank you for all the blessed teaching of your holy Word concerning our children. We thank you that it has set them before us in your light, as created by you, though ruined by sin, redeemed in Christ, and now entrusted to us to keep and care for, while the Holy Spirit renews them to your eternal life and glory. We thank you for coming as our teacher to equip us for teaching them. We pray for your blessing on each word of yours, that we may become the parents you would have us to be.

Lord, we pray, establish in our thoughts and hearts and lives all the wonderful truths that apply to the home. We count your covenants and its promises very precious. Our faith sees the names you have given our children: children of the covenant, children of the promise, and children of the kingdom, as written on their foreheads. We would treasure all the promises of your Spirit and your blessing as their sacred heritage. We accept your warnings and instructions concerning children as the laws of our home. Open our eyes that we may ever have before us the picture of a believing home as you will it to be—as you will to make it for us.

Above all, blessed Lord Jesus, let your presence and your love and your joy, filling our hearts, be the power to fulfill the Father's will and to see our children's salvation. Come into our home and make it a place where you love to stay. Then shall it be truly blessed, full of gladness and hope. Amen.